A COOK'S BOOK OF

quick
fixes

ANNE WILLAN

How to turn adversity into
opportunity

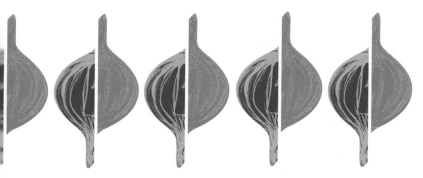

ILLUSTRATIONS BY JANET SIMON

QUADRILLE

CONTENTS

INTRODUCTION

After over 35 eventful years in the kitchen, I have developed a series of taste-saving devices, such as a tablespoon of Cognac, a squeeze of citrus juice or a few drops of soy sauce; together with little sauces and relishes, such as the escabèche marinade for overcooked fish on page 12-13 and the yoghurt and herb dressing for vegetables on page 106. Whipped cream can hide a multitude of sins in desserts and chopped parsley will do the same for savoury dishes. To provide you with fixes for all eventualities, I have suggested lots of cheerful garnishes for poor-looking food and appropriate seasonings for bland food, as well as remedies for technical problems like curdled mayonnaise or sticky pastry dough. With the possible exceptions of oversalting and scorching (see the next page), there are surprisingly few things that cannot be saved if you really try.

ANNE WILLAN

THE PERILS OF OVERSALTING
AND SCORCHING

The two faults in cooking that are the most difficult to cure are oversalting and scorching. Remedies for too much salt depend on whether the food is raw or cooked. You can extract salt from small pieces of raw food, such as olives or diced bacon, by blanching them. Put them in a pan of cold water, bring them slowly to the boil, then drain and rinse them. Ingredients that are large and/or very salty, such as a whole ham or fillets of salt cod, require more lengthy treatment by soaking in several changes of cold water over several hours, or even a day or two. Too much salt in finished dishes, such as a stew or a sauce, can be counteracted by adding a bland ingredient like potato, tomato, mushroom, or a dairy product such as cream, milk or fresh cheese.

Burnt food is hard to disguise. When food is scorched on the surface, it is relatively easy to scrape off the burned portion, as for toast or pastry.

When a sauce or stew catches on the base of the pan, spoon out the rest, leaving the burned residue behind – on no account stir, as this will mix burned and unburned food. If the burning has been severe, however, a smoky taste pervades the whole dish and little can be done.

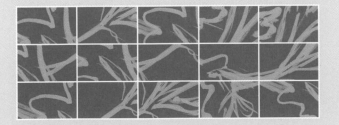

FISH &

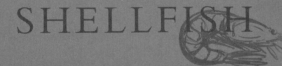

SHELLFISH

A FLAVOURSOME BLANKET TO COVER DRY FISH FILLETS

Here's a colourful topping to moisten dry fish fillets and pick up their flavour: squeeze the juice of 1 lemon or lime into a bowl; add 2 tomatoes, seeded and chopped but not peeled, then 2 stalks of very thinly sliced celery, and finally 2 tablespoons coarsely chopped dill or parsley. Moisten this with 1 tablespoon vegetable oil if you like. Season with salt and pepper and sprinkle topping over fillets. Serves 4.

MAKE AN ESCABECHE TO SAVE OVERCOOKED FISH

Unless already in a sauce, turn dry or overcooked fish steaks into marinated escabeche. In a food processor or blender, combine 1 small onion cut into pieces, 1 peeled garlic clove, pared zest of 1 orange and 1 lemon, handful of parsley, 2 teaspoons paprika, pinch of cayenne, salt and pepper. Work to a coarse purée.

Add 125 ml/4 fl oz olive oil and 3 tablespoons red wine vinegar and work

again until smooth. Spread fish in a dish while still warm and spoon over the marinade. Serve at once if you like, but preferably cover tightly and refrigerate at least 8 hours. Enough for 1 kg/2 pounds of fish fillets, to serve 4-6.

A PIQUANT DRESSING TO
SOAK INTO DRY FISH

Pretend overcooking or dryness of the fish is deliberate so flesh will absorb more of the following dressing.

In a food processor or blender, combine 2 tablespoons lemon juice, 2 tablespoons white wine vinegar, 1 tablespoon chopped fresh ginger, 1 shallot, coarsely chopped, 1 tablespoon Dijon-style mustard, ¼ teaspoon freshly grated nutmeg, salt and pepper. In a slow steady stream, pour in 175 ml/6 fl oz olive oil, so the dressing emulsifies and thickens slightly. Taste for seasoning before spooning over the fish. Makes about 250 ml/8 fl oz, to serve 4. The fish may be served hot or at room temperature.

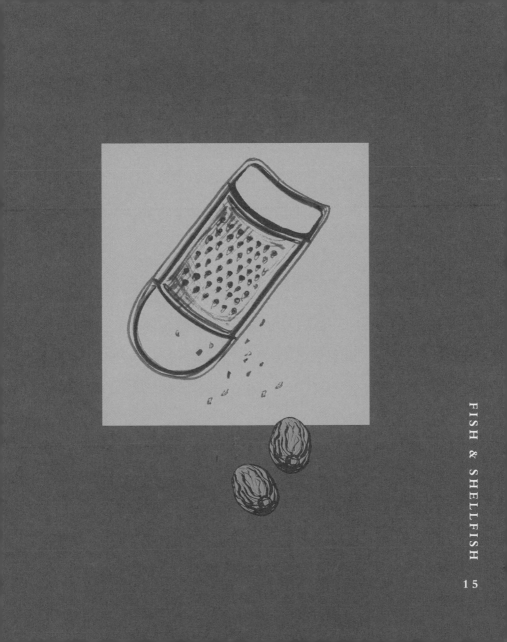

DEEP-FRY SOME HERBS TO DISTRACT FROM POOR DEEP-FRIED FISH OR SHELLFISH

While the hot oil cools slightly, rinse a large bunch of parsley, detach sprigs and dry them thoroughly on paper towels. Wash a bunch of basil and/or sage, detach and dry leaves. Toss a handful of parsley into the fat, fry about 30 seconds until sputtering stops and at once scoop out with a wire scoop or basket. Repeat for the remaining herbs. Sprinkle over fish and serve.

TRANSFORM OVERCOOKED SEAFOOD STEWS INTO A SOUP

Remove pieces of fish and shellfish from the liquid, discard skin and bones and set shellfish aside. Purée fish in 2-3 batches with a little liquid. Pour into a soup pan, add remaining liquid, bring to the boil and season with cayenne, salt and pepper. If very thick, thin with a little cream, milk or water. Replace shellfish, heat gently and taste, adding white wine, lemon juice, tomato purée or cayenne as you like. Serve with croutons.

A CRISP VEGETABLE TOPPING TO ZIP UP A SECOND-RATE SEAFOOD STIR-FRY

For overcooked or tasteless stir-fries, I would suggest you use a crispy vegetable topping to counteract softness and lack of flavour.

Tip the stir-fried ingredients into a strainer and discard any liquid. Transfer them to a bowl and keep warm. Using a food processor or mandoline cutter, thinly slice 1-2 courgettes or yellow squash. Clean and dry the wok, heat 2.5-5 cm/1-2 inches of vegetable oil to sizzling hot and add the vegetable slices one at a time so they do not stick. Do not crowd the pan. Stir-fry for 2-3 minutes, stirring constantly until the slices are deep golden brown. Remove with a slotted spoon and drain on paper towels. Fry more in the same way. Sprinkle slices with salt and scatter over the stir-fry.

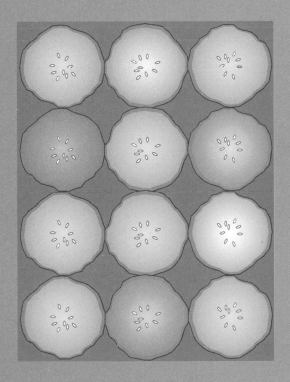

DARING DRESSINGS
TO DISTRACT
FROM DULL PÂTÉS
AND MOUSSES

Mask problems by coating pâté or mousseline
with one of these dressings:

- Whisk together 250ml/8floz plain yogurt,
  3 tablespoons chopped chives, grated zest
  of 2 lemons or 2 limes, juice of 1 lemon,

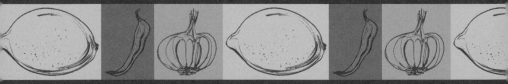

2 tablespoons mayonnaise, salt and a large pinch of cayenne or a few drops of Tabasco. Season to taste. Makes about 375 ml/12 fl oz, to serve 3-4.

• For an Oriental flavour: in a bowl, combine the grated zest of 1 lemon, 1 chopped stalk of lemon grass, 2 chopped garlic cloves, ½ green chilli pepper, deseeded and chopped, the juice of 3 limes, 60 ml/2 fl oz (nam pla) fish sauce and 2 tablespoons sugar. Stir well until the sugar dissolves completely.

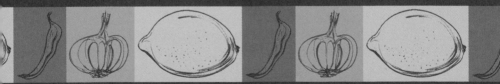

A CLASSIC THERMIDOR
SAUCE FOR BLAND LOBSTER

When lobster is not up to standard, traditionally chefs resort to the classic Thermidor sauce.

For each lobster, melt 1 tablespoon butter in a saucepan and sauté 1 chopped shallot until soft. Whisk in 1 tablespoon flour and cook until foaming. Whisk in 175 ml/6 fl oz double cream and bring to the boil, whisking constantly until the sauce thickens. Simmer 1 minute. Take from heat and stir in 2 tablespoons white wine, 2 tablespoons grated Parmesan cheese, 1 teaspoon Dijon-style mustard and 1 tablespoon chopped tarragon or 2 teaspoons dried tarragon. Season to taste. If the lobster is served whole, use the sauce for dipping. If the lobster is split, spoon the sauce over the halves. Sprinkle with a little more Parmesan and grill until brown, 1–2 minutes. Serves 1–2

FISH & SHELLFISH

A CRAB SALAD TO COMBAT
LACK OF FLAVOUR

Crab is good combined in a salad with orange, grapefruit, tomato or green pepper – all colourful distractions from mediocre meat.

Mix 500 g/1 pound crab meat with this sauce: combine 125 ml/4 fl oz mayonnaise, 4 tablespoons sour cream and the juice of 1 orange. Peel and slice 2 oranges, or 1 large grapefruit, and 2 large tomatoes. Core and seed 1 red or green pepper and cut it across into rings. Arrange the orange or grapefruit and tomato slices overlapping on 6 individual plates. Pile the crab meat on top and decorate with the pepper rings. Serves 6 as an appetizer or 4 as a light main course.

A QUICK SEAFOOD
SALAD TO MAKE
THE MOST OF
BLAND SHELLFISH

If I suspect shrimp, prawns or crayfish are bland, I often make a quick seafood salad.

For every 375 g/¾ pound peeled, cooked, chopped shellfish, combine about 150 g/5 oz chopped celery, 125 ml/4 fl oz mayonnaise, 1 medium onion, finely chopped, 3–4 coarsely chopped hard-boiled eggs, the juice of ½ lemon, ½ teaspoon paprika, salt and pepper. Add the shellfish and stir to mix. Season to taste and pile on a bed of salad greens. Serves 3-4.

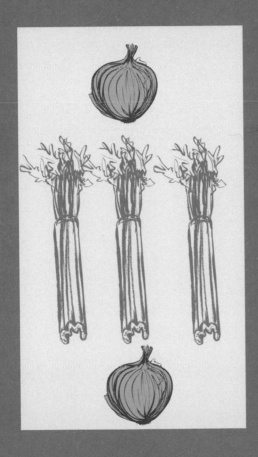

STUFFED PANCAKES TO SALVAGE OVERCOOKED SEAFOOD

Chop overcooked shellfish and make pancakes. For every 175 g/6 oz chopped cooked shellfish, sift together 125 g/4 oz plain flour, 1¾ teaspoons baking powder, ½ teaspoon salt, ½ teaspoon sugar and ¼ teaspoon ground black pepper. Strain clam or mussel liquid through muslin or a fine sieve and measure 60 ml/2 fl oz. Make a well in the centre of the flour and add the measured liquid with 175 ml/6 fl oz milk, 2 teaspoons melted butter and 1 egg. Stir with a whisk until mixed, then gradually draw in flour to form a smooth batter. Stir in the chopped clams or mussels with 1 tablespoon chopped thyme. In a 10-cm/4-inch frying pan, heat 15-30 g/½-1 oz butter until foaming. Using a ladle, add 2-3 tablespoons batter to form a pancake. Fry this briskly until it is firm and browned, 2-3 minutes, flip and brown the other side. Fry the remaining pancakes, adding more butter as needed. Serve with some sour cream. Makes about 10-12 pancakes, to serve 4-6.

A CITRUSY PASTA SALAD TO SAVE SAD SCALLOPS

Dress scallops which are overcooked, tough or tasteless as a pasta salad.

For 750 g/1$\frac{1}{2}$ pounds scallops, cook 500 g/1 pound coloured or tri-coloured pasta such as shells or fusilli. In a small bowl, combine the juice of 3 lemons, 2 limes and 1 orange. Whisk in 5 tablespoons vegetable oil and 30 g/1 oz coarsely chopped parsley. Drain any sauce from the scallops and cut them across in thin rounds to minimize toughness. Add to the pasta, pour over the dressing and toss to mix. Season to taste. Serves 4.

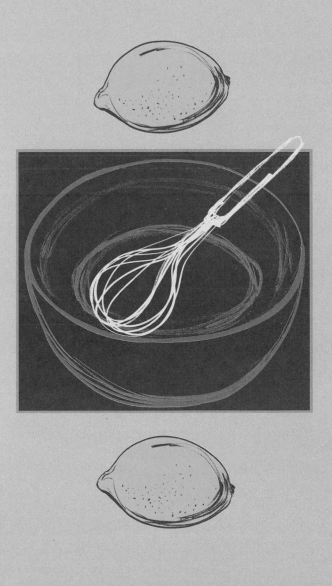

A PASTA SAUCE TO RESCUE TOUGH SHELLFISH

Overcooked clams and mussels are inedibly tough. The only answer is to shell and chop them, discarding the neck of clams or rubbery ring around mussels, then add them to pasta. For 175 g/6 oz chopped cooked shellfish, cook 250 g/½ pound of pasta. Strain clam or mussel liquid and add water to make 250 ml/8 fl oz.

In a frying pan, heat 2 tablespoons olive oil, add 2 chopped garlic cloves and sauté for 30 seconds. Add cooking liquid, 125 ml/4 fl oz double cream, pinch of nutmeg and pepper. Simmer over high heat until slightly thickened and sauce coats a spoon. Stir in shellfish, 30 g/1 oz chopped parsley and 30 g/1 oz chopped stoned black olives. Toss with pasta. Serves 2.

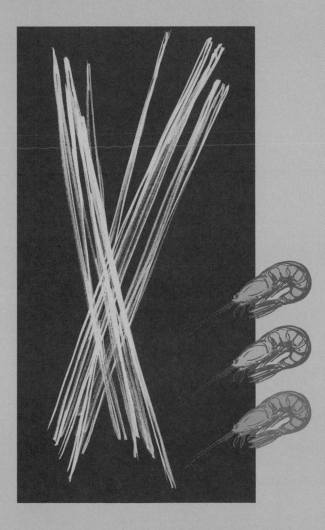

FISH & SHELLFISH

35

POULTRY

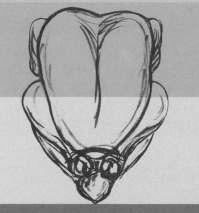

&GAME

AN ORIENTAL GLAZE FOR DULL ROAST CHICKEN

For simply roasted chicken that is dry and overcooked or bland: brush the hot cooked bird with an Oriental mix of 2 tablespoons soy sauce, 2 teaspoons dark sesame oil, 1 garlic clove, finely chopped, 1 tablespoon chopped fresh ginger, juice of ½ lime and 1 tablespoon chopped fresh coriander. Add an Oriental accompaniment of stir-fried green beans with sesame oil.

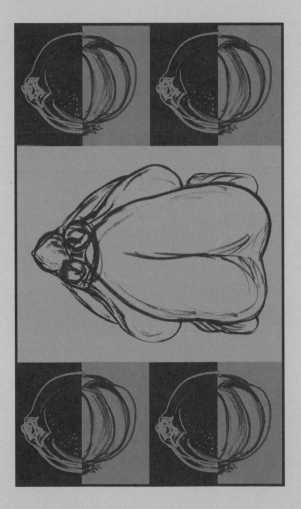

A CHICKEN SALAD TO USE UP SECOND-RATE COOKED POULTRY

Transform overcooked or bland chicken into chicken salad: cut the meat from the carcass and tear or cut it into large shreds. For about 1 pound/500 g of cooked chicken, combine in a bowl 2 tablespoons Dijon-style mustard, 30 g/1 oz chopped tarragon, parsley or chives, 30 g/1 oz toasted flaked almonds, 375 g/12 oz halved seedless grapes and 175 ml/6 fl oz mayonnaise. Add the chicken and stir to mix. Add more mayonnaise if you like and season to taste with salt and pepper.
Serves 4-6.

DRESSING PLATES OF LESS-THAN-PERFECT TURKEY TO DISTRACT

Draw attention away from the bird by decorating the platter with tomato baskets filled with diced celery or cucumber for a crisp contrast. For a lavish approach, pile on some grilled cocktail sausages and little rolls of crispy bacon. Disguise problems with the bird itself – skin not browned, split or scorched – with sprigs of watercress, branches of herbs, even a strategically placed flower or two. Purists may frown, but turkey is a celebration and the situation calls for a touch of fantasy.

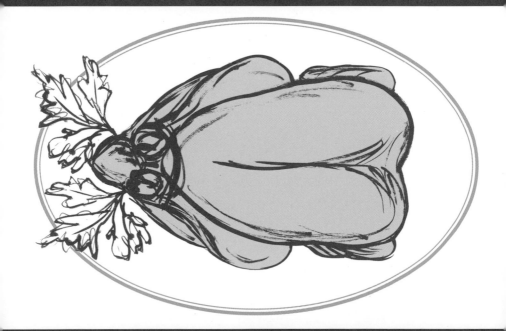

A SPICY COATING FOR BLAND BIRDS

Try this spicy coating for bland or overcooked poultry pieces, no matter the bird or how cooked. First drain any sauce and reserve. Brush the poultry with oil. For 6-8 pieces, combine 60 g/2 oz dry brown or white breadcrumbs, 2 teaspoons dry mustard,

1 teaspoon ground ginger, 1 teaspoon ground allspice, 1 teaspoon ground black pepper, a large pinch of grated nutmeg and ½ teaspoon ground hot red pepper, or more to taste, and pour into a large plastic bag. Add poultry pieces, close bag and shake vigorously to coat with spiced breadcrumbs. Lay pieces on an oiled baking sheet and grill for 3-5 minutes each side until browned, turning once. Reheat any sauce and serve separately.

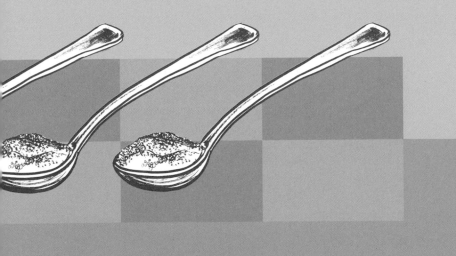

PAIR POOR POULTRY BREASTS WITH CRISP VEGETABLES IN AN ENERGETIC STIR-FRY

I often rely on the crisp vegetables and energetic flavourings of a good stir-fry to revive cooked chicken breast.

Cut the breasts into thin strips. For every 375 g/12 oz cooked meat, mix 2 tablespoons dark soy sauce, 2 tablespoons rice wine, a pinch of sugar and 2 teaspoons cornflour. Mix with chicken and leave to marinate.

Heat 2 tablespoons oil in a wok. Add 6 chopped spring onions, 2 small dried chillies, a 2.5-cm/1-inch piece of fresh ginger, finely chopped, and 1 garlic clove, finely chopped. Stir-fry until fragrant, about 30 seconds.

Add 250 g / ½ pound shredded bok choy or white cabbage and stir-fry until beginning to soften, about 1 minute. Drain chicken, reserving marinade, and add to wok. Stir-fry until very hot, about 2 minutes. Add marinade to wok, stirring constantly until marinade thickens and coats chicken and peas. Discard chilli peppers, taste for seasoning and serve at once. Serves 4

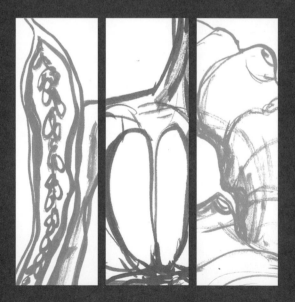

SERVE A LACKLUSTRE POULTRY STIR-FRY IN NESTS OF DEEP-FRIED NOODLES

Hopefully, no one will pay much attention to a faulty stir-fry if you serve it in a nest of deep-fried noodles.

In a wok, heat about 5 cm/2 inches vegetable oil until a noodle sizzles when added. Break a handful of dried bean thread noodles into 13-cm/5-inch lengths and, with a slotted spoon, lower into hot fat. At once slide out the spoon and press it down on noodles so they are immersed. Fry until puffed and crisp, 30-60 seconds. Lift out and drain on paper towels. Fry more nests, one for each person.

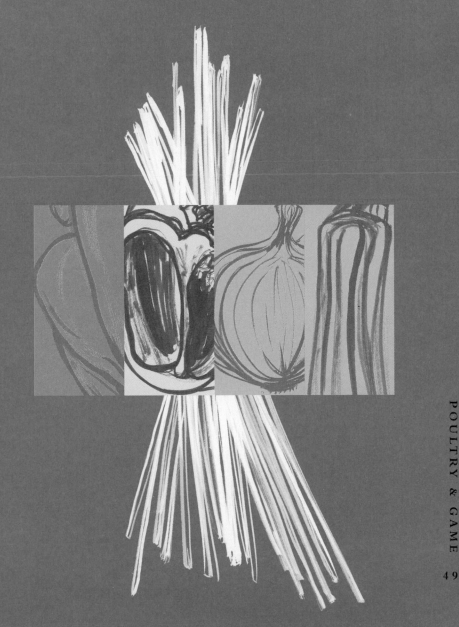

A SWEET-AND-SOUR DRESSING FOR DISAPPOINTING DUCK AND GOOSE

Distract attention from disappointing duck or goose with this colourful salad in a sweet-and-sour dressing.

Core 4 large tomatoes and thinly slice them. Cut the peel and skin from 4 large oranges and thinly slice them across. Interleave tomato and orange slices on 4 salad plates. In a small bowl, whisk together 4 tablespoons port, 2 tablespoons raspberry vinegar, 2 tablespoons lemon juice, 1 tablespoon honey, and salt and pepper to taste. Spoon dressing over fruits and top each plate with a mint sprig. Serves 4.

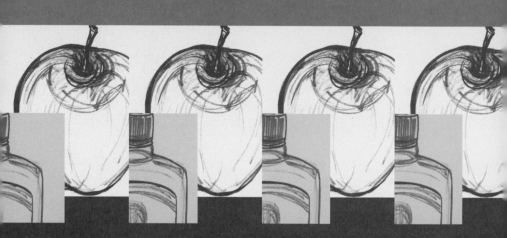

CALVADOS–FLAMED CARAMELIZED APPLES TO DISGUISE POOR DUCK OR GAME

When duck or game bird breasts are dry, tough or overcooked, apple provides moisture and blends with almost any sauce. Drain breasts, reserving any juices. Thinly slice meat on the diagonal, cutting across the grain,

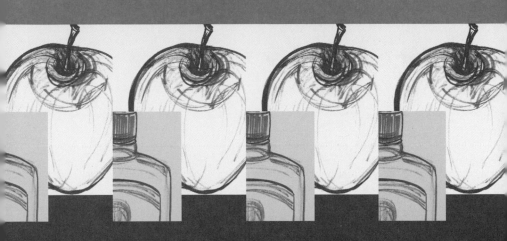

arrange on plates and keep warm. For 4 people, quarter, core and slice 3 tart apples. Melt 2 tablespoons butter in a frying pan, add apples and sprinkle with 1 tablespoon sugar. Turn slices and sprinkle with 1 tablespoon more sugar. Sauté slices until brown and caramelized. Turn and brown other sides. Add 2-3 tablespoons Calvados or Cognac and flame. Add any reserved juices, taste and spoon apples over breasts.

A DEVIL OF A DIPPING SAUCE
FOR DRY GAME BIRDS

Small birds are often deliberately cooked until
dry to act as foil for a dipping sauce like this
one. In a small saucepan, combine
4 tablespoons tomato ketchup, 3 tablespoons
red wine vinegar, 30 g/1 oz butter,
1 tablespoon brown sugar, and a dash of
Tabasco. Bring mixture to the boil, stirring,
and taste, adding more ·Tabasco if you like.
Brush sauce over birds and serve the rest on
the side as a dipping sauce. Enough for
4 small birds, to serve 4.

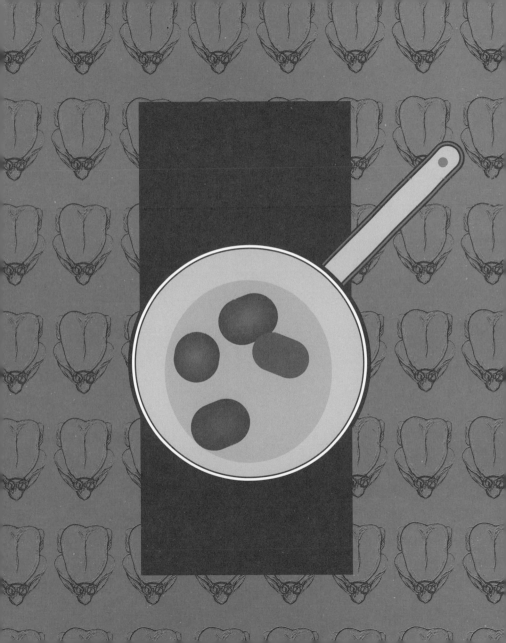

BACON MASH AS A FOIL FOR DRY GAME BIRDS

Bacon mashed potatoes act as foil for a dry or overcooked bird (and be sure to make plenty of gravy or sauce). Allow a medium potato per person and, to speed cooking, bring a pan of water to the boil. Meanwhile, thickly slice the potatoes without peeling them. Add to the water and simmer until very tender,

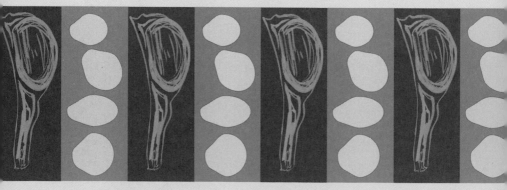

10-15 minutes. Dice 1 thick slice of bacon per person and fry until browned. Drain on paper towel, reserving the fat. Drain the potatoes, return them to the pan and dry over low heat, 1-2 minutes. Mash with a potato masher in the pan. For each potato, add 1 tablespoon reserved bacon fat with 2 tablespoons milk and beat over low heat with a wooden spoon until the potatoes are fluffy, 3-5 minutes. Beat in the bacon bits and season with pepper and salt if needed.

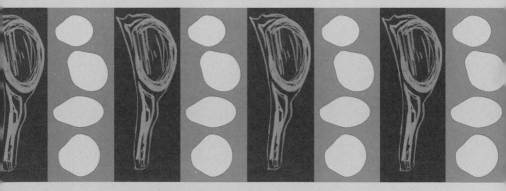

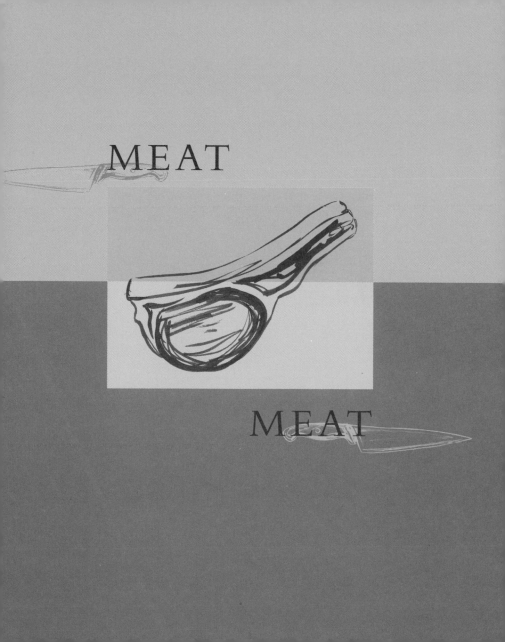

TASTY ITALIAN VEGETABLE SOFFRITO TO PERK UP ROAST MEAT

A soffrito is a classic base for many Italian dishes and a wonderful savoury condiment in itself for roast meats. Cut 2 onions in pieces and add to a food processor with 2 peeled garlic cloves. Work with the pulse button until quite coarsely chopped. Transfer to a bowl. Cut 2 stalks of celery and 2 peeled carrots in pieces and chop them also in the processor. Remove and combine with the onion and 125 ml/4 fl oz olive oil. Transfer to a saucepan and season with salt and pepper. Sauté, stirring often, until the vegetables are soft, translucent and just beginning to brown, 10-12 minutes. Taste for seasoning. Serves 4-6.

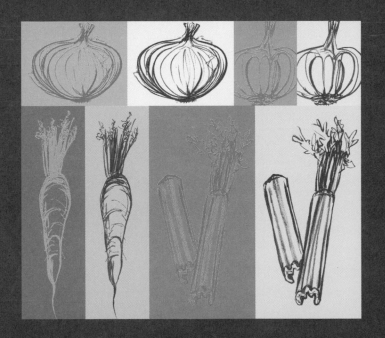

A TOMATO, GARLIC AND BASIL
SALSA TO MASK BLAND MEAT

I make this raw tomato, garlic and basil salsa often as a punchy condiment to cover blandness in everything from meat and poultry to fish.

In a small bowl, whisk together 5 tablespoons balsamic vinegar, 3 chopped garlic cloves, salt and pepper. Gradually whisk in 150 ml/ 5 fl oz olive oil so the dressing emulsifies and thickens slightly. Core and halve 3 tomatoes and squeeze out the seeds. Chop the halves and stir into the dressing with the shredded leaves from a small bunch of basil. Taste for seasoning. Makes 250 ml/8 fl oz, to serve 4.

SHRED SECOND-RATE COOKED MEAT FOR A ZINGY SALAD

When cooking has been a bit 'haphazard', I often shred meats for a salad. For every 375 g/¾ pound shredded or thinly sliced meat, mix 1 tablespoon Dijon-style mustard, 1 tablespoon coarse-grain mustard, 2 finely chopped shallots, salt and pepper in a medium bowl. Gradually whisk in 125 ml/4 fl oz olive oil so the dressing emulsifies. Add the meat, stir until coated and season to taste. Serves 4.

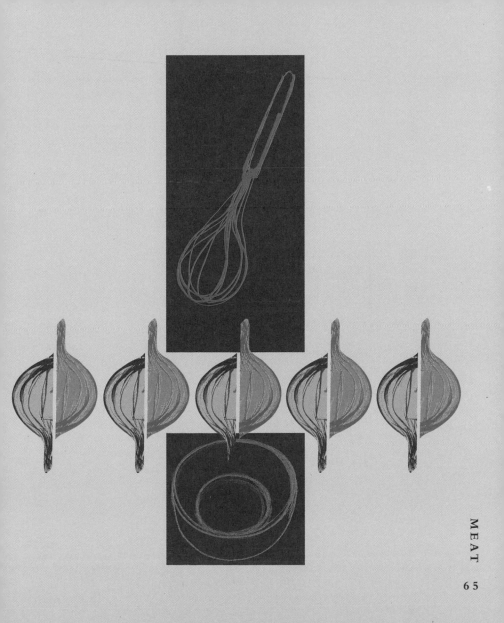

MEAT

GIVE BLAND BEEF THE 'AU POIVRE' TREATMENT

As every chef knows, the sauce for classic steak au poivre is an excellent cover-up for beef that is overcooked, tough, or lacking in flavour.

Put 2 tablespoons whole black peppercorns in a plastic bag and crush with a heavy pan or rolling pin, or use 1½ tablespoons cracked pepper. Add pepper to 175 ml/6 fl oz red

wine and boil until reduced to 2 tablespoons. Whisk in 175 ml/6 fl oz double cream and 1 tablespoon Cognac and season to taste with salt. Serves 2 generously.

A SIMPLE STEW TO SAVE
TOUGH VEAL CHOPS

For tough or overcooked veal medallions or chops, heat a tablespoon of oil or 15 g/½ oz butter in a frying pan and sauté a thinly sliced onion until brown. Lay 2 medallions or chops on top and add stock to cover. Cover the pan

and simmer until the meat is very tender when pierced with a two-pronged fork, 15-20 minutes for veal medallions and 30-40 minutes for chops. Remove meat and keep warm. Add 2-3 thinly sliced mushrooms and simmer until sauce is full-flavoured, 5-7 minutes. Add 1-2 tablespoons of cream, a tablespoon of Madeira, sherry or sweet white wine, and a few chopped herbs to taste. Spoon over meat. Serves 2.

REFRESHING TABBOULEH, THE PERFECT FOIL FOR ANY MEAT IN SAUCE

Tunisian tabbouleh salad makes a really refreshing accompaniment to any dish of meat in sauce. Pour 250 ml/8 fl oz boiling water over 175 g/6 oz instant couscous with 1 teaspoon salt, stir and leave to soak. Pare zest

of 2 lemons, halve zest strips and purée in food processor with juice from lemons. Cut 1 onion into pieces and combine in processor with leaves from large bunches of mint and parsley. Using pulse button, purée until chunky. Pour over couscous. Core and halve 3 tomatoes. Squeeze out seeds, dice halves small and add to couscous. Pour over 175 ml/6 fl oz olive oil and toss. Season to taste. Serves 4-6.

A SIMPLE TRICK TO GIVE BODY AND COLOUR TO A MEAT STEW

When sauce for a meat stew lacks body or colour, stir in 2–3 teaspoons tomato purée.

A QUICK ·SALSA TO HELP BLAND MINCE

For overcooked or bland minced meat, make up a quick tomato salsa. Cut 500 g/1 pound fresh plum tomatoes in halves, squeeze to remove seeds and chop the halves. Then mix with 2-3 tablespoons red wine vinegar, 2 chopped garlic cloves, salt, pepper and lots and lots of chopped mint. Serves 4.

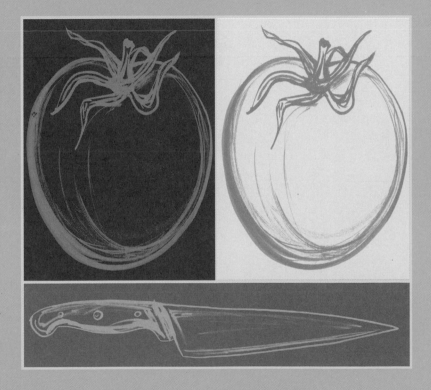

CRISP AND TASTY EDIBLE GARNISHES TO DISTRACT FROM TIRED TERRINES

Garnish individual plates of a terrine that is dry or overcooked with a cornucopia of raw vegetables, such as radishes and carrot, celery and courgette, cut into sticks. If serving the terrine on a platter, arrange slices overlapping to mask damage and surround them with piles or bouquets of raw vegetables. Add a variety of olives, marinated peppers, artichoke hearts or okra, if you like, and don't forget your favourite mustard.

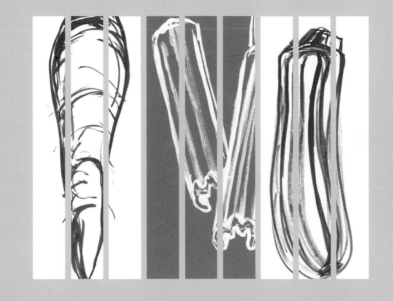

A CRUNCHY SHALLOT
TOPPING FOR STEAKS

A crisp topping of chopped shallots is the
favourite way with steak in the Bordeaux
region of France. The texture and piquant
flavour will distract from blandness, dryness or
toughness. Try it, too, with steaks of fish such
as tuna and swordfish.

Grill or fry your steaks and warm a heatproof
serving dish until very hot. Peel and chop
2 shallots per person. When the steaks are
cooked, sprinkle half of them in the hot
serving dish. Set the steaks on top, sprinkle
with the rest of the shallots, and serve. Juices
from the steaks will moisten the shallots, but
they will still be crunchy.

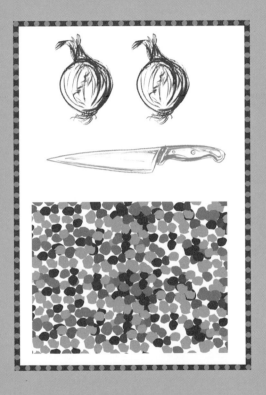

A HONEY-MUSTARD SAUCE TO PERK UP TIRED PORK

For dry, tired pork, make this honey mustard sauce. In a small bowl, combine 3 tablespoons finely chopped dill, 2 tablespoons whole-grain mustard, 2 tablespoons honey, 1 tablespoon Dijon-style mustard and 1 tablespoon sugar. Stir until mixed. Makes 75 ml/2$\frac{1}{2}$ fl oz sauce, to serve 4.

A PAPRIKA SAUCE TO HELP COUNTERACT OVER-SALTY HAM

For dry or salty cooked ham make this paprika sauce: melt 15 g/$\frac{1}{2}$ oz butter in a large frying pan and sauté 1 sliced onion until soft. Add 1 tablespoon paprika and cook gently, stirring constantly, 1 minute. Add 2-3 tablespoons vodka and flame. Stir in 250 ml/8 fl oz double cream and bring to the boil. Add ham and heat gently until hot, basting well. Taste for seasoning. Serves 4.

CHEESE-STUFFED CHILLIES
GIVE PLAIN GRILLS ZIP

The pocket in a chilli pepper just asks for stuffing, and the simplest stuffing of all is a piece of cheese. The heat of the finished dish will depend on the type of chilli, whether it be a jalapeño or serrano, or any one of the many types now available. Serve these little nuggets as a lively accompaniment to grills, particularly pork chops, sausages, and chicken.

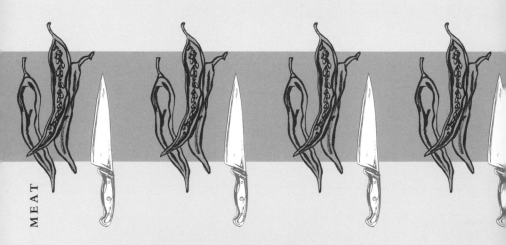

MEAT

80

Preheat the oven to 175°C/350°F/gas4. Allow 1-2 chillies per person. Slit them down one side and scoop out the cores and seeds. From a piece of mild Cheddar cheese, cut strips that are the same length as the chillies. Stuff the cheese strips into the chillies. Pour 2-3 tablespoons olive oil into a small baking dish, add the chillies and turn them so they are well coated with oil. Cover with foil and bake in the oven until the chillies are tender, 25-30 minutes.

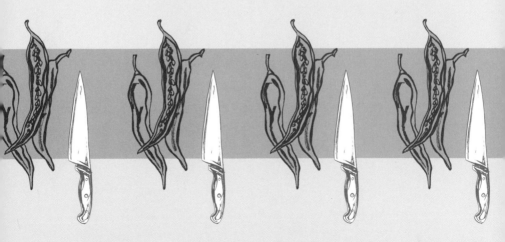

A SWEET-HOT TOPPING TO MASK POOR HAM

To help ham that is wet, stringy, salty or bland, add a sweet-hot topping. If not already done, score the ham fat deeply in a lattice pattern.

For a ham for 6-8 people, mix 4 tablespoons Dijon-style mustard and 100 g/3¼ oz dark brown sugar to a paste and spread over fat. Spear the centre of each diamond in the lattice with a whole clove. Roast ham in a 200°C/400°F/gas6 oven, basting every few minutes, until the sugar is melted and the surface a rich dark brown, 15-20 minutes.

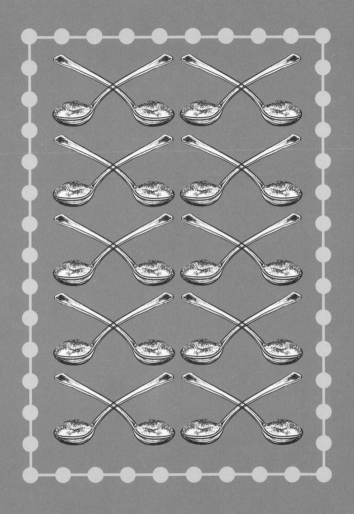

RED RADISH RELISH ENLIVENS MEATS NOT QUITE IN THE PINK

This little Italian recipe is perfect with any meats that need a bit of help with colour and crunch, and it also goes well with cold chicken and pork – even salmon! The sliced radishes turn a happy pink when marinated in salt and lemon juice, and they last well in the refrigerator for several days.

Trim 450 g/1 lb red radishes, then slice them as thinly as possible, using a mandoline grater, if you have one, for large radishes. Put the slices in a bowl with $\frac{1}{2}$ teaspoon salt and the juice of 1 lemon. Mix well and chill for at least an hour. Stir, taste the radishes and adjust the seasoning if necessary.

EGGS

EGGS

EGG MAYONNAISE AS A FACE-SAVER FOR OVERCOOKED OR UNTIDY EGGS

Egg mayonnaise is a face-saver for overdone mollet or hard-boiled eggs, or for untidy eggs which burst in the pan or are hard to peel. Coarsely chop the eggs and mix with some mayonnaise, allowing 125 ml/4 fl oz for every 6 eggs. Stir in 30 g/1 oz chopped herbs and 2 finely chopped spring onions. Season to taste. Serve on toast with crisp lettuce leaves.

SERVE OVERCOOKED OR RAGGED POACHED EGGS IN BLANCHED LETTUCE LEAVES

For poached eggs which are overcooked or with untidy whites: for each egg, blanch a large lettuce leaf in boiling salted water for 20–30 seconds. Remove, refresh under cold running water and pat dry with paper towels. Wrap a leaf around each egg. Serve plain or with whatever sauce was intended.

USE A PASTRY CUTTER TO TIDY RAGGED FRIED EGGS

For untidy or overcooked eggs, trim egg with a pastry cutter to neaten the white and remove scorched edges.

TURN A LESS-THAN-PERFECT OMELETTE INTO A SANDWICH FILLING

If a flat omelette is overcooked, falls apart or looks unattractive, use it as filling for a sandwich on baguette or pitta bread.

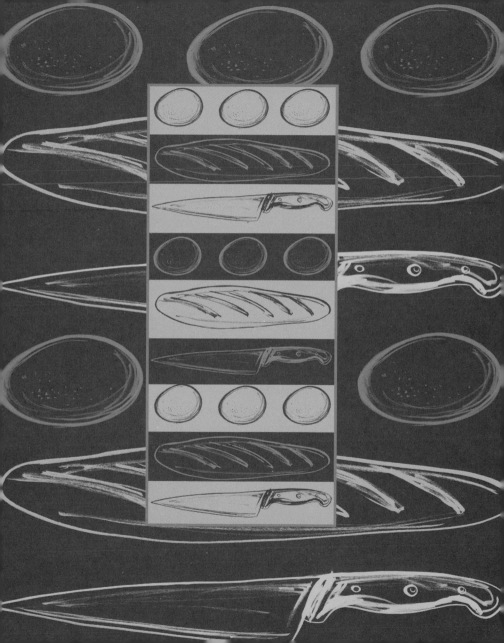

RESCUING AN OMELETTE THAT'S OVERCOOKED OR STUCK TO THE PAN

For an omelette which is overcooked or sticks to the pan: leave omelette flat in the pan, moisten it with 2-3 tablespoons double cream and sprinkle with grated cheese. Grill until browned, 1-2 minutes. To serve, cut omelette in wedges like a cake.

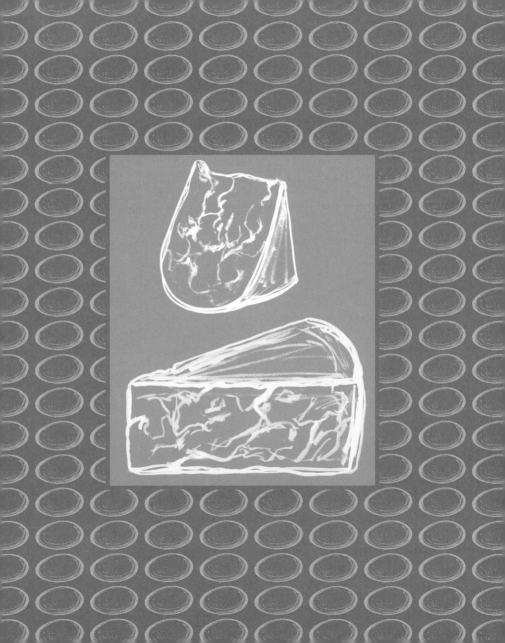

RESCUING SEPARATED OR WATERY SCRAMBLED EGGS

For stiff, separated or watery scrambled eggs: for each serving portion, toast a slice of white bread or round of French bread. Cut 6-cm/2½-inch rounds from the warm toast and brush with melted butter or oil. With an ice cream scoop or two tablespoons, shape balls of scrambled egg and set on the toast rounds. Top with crossed slivers of pimento, smoked salmon or a slice of truffle.

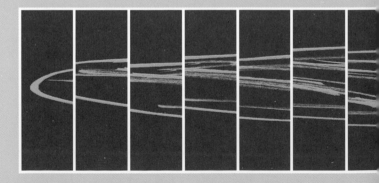

DISGUISING OVERCOOKED EGGS

To disguise overcooked eggs: moisten them with a spoonful of double cream or drizzle of melted butter or walnut oil and top with a sprig of basil, two crossed chive stems or a halved black olive.

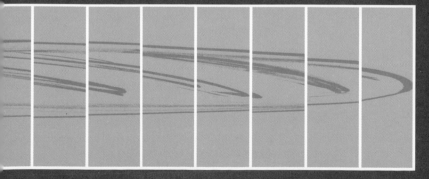

SERVING A SUNKEN SOUFFLÉ WITH STYLE

There is no quick fix for a fallen soufflé; the cook just has to brazen it out. Serve collapsed savoury soufflé with a green salad, if possible cutting the mixture into wedges like quiche Lorraine. Serve a fallen sweet soufflé like a pudding, topping it with whipped cream or ice cream.

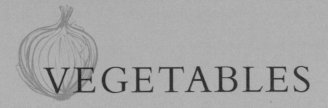

VEGETABLES

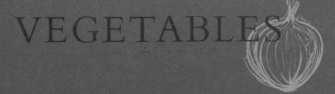

VEGETABLES

DISGUISING OVERCOOKED OR DISCOLOURED ARTICHOKES

When an artichoke is overcooked or discoloured, pull away large plump leaves and arrange in concentric circles on a large individual plate. Discard the central leaves and the small outer leaves as well as the choke. Set the artichoke bottom in the centre of a plate. Spoon a little tomato salsa (page 72), using chopped coriander leaves instead of mint, or some mayonnaise or hollandaise sauce into the artichoke bottom, serving the remaining sauce separately.

MAKE ASPARAGUS VINAIGRETTE TO MASK OVERCOOKED SPEARS

When asparagus is a bit overcooked, dress it as a vinaigrette salad. Cut the spears at an angle into 1-cm/$\frac{3}{8}$-inch slices, reserving tips. For every 250 g/8 oz sliced asparagus, thinly slice 3 celery stalks or $\frac{1}{2}$ fennel bulb. Add 3-4 tablespoons chopped fresh tarragon and vinaigrette dressing made with 1 teaspoon Dijon-style mustard, 2 tablespoons lemon juice, 5 tablespoons olive oil, salt and pepper. Mix gently, taste and adjust the seasoning. Pile the salad on individual plates or in a serving bowl and top with asparagus tips. Serves 2-3.

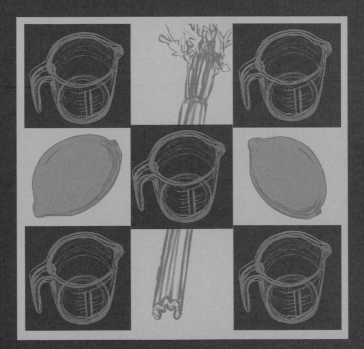

SAVE LESS-THAN-PERFECT GREENS BY CREAMING THEM

All of these green vegetables are difficult to save when they've gone wrong. Simplest is to transform them into a creamed vegetable: to 375 g/¾ pound cooked, sliced vegetable add

45 g/1½ oz butter, salt and pepper and a generous grating of nutmeg. Cover and sauté for 3-4 minutes. Uncover and cook until almost dry, 3-4 minutes. Add 125 ml/4 fl oz double cream and cook over a medium heat, stirring often, until soft and creamy, 7-10 minutes. Season to taste. Serves 4.

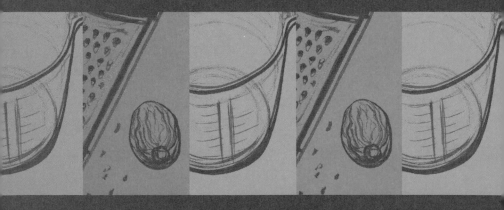

MEDITERRANEAN-STYLE YOGHURT DRESSING TO PERK UP SECOND-RATE VEGETABLES

Revive any tired vegetables with this Mediterranean-style yoghurt dressing.

For every 375 g/¾ pound of drained cooked vegetables combine 125 ml/4 fl oz plain yoghurt, 1 tablespoon chopped dill, 1 tablespoon chopped mixed herbs such as coriander, mint, parsley or tarragon, large pinch of ground cinnamon, the juice of ½ lemon and a pinch of sugar. Mix well. Pour the dressing over the drained vegetables and toss well. Season to taste. Serves 4.

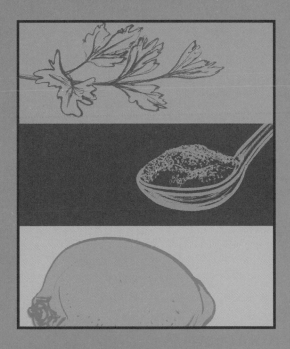

107

TURN LACKLUSTRE BROCCOLI AND CAULIFLOWER INTO A SIMPLE TASTY SOUP

To save bland or overcooked broccoli or cauliflower, make them into a soup. Allow about 500 ml/16 fl oz chicken or vegetable stock for every 375 g/¾ pound cooked broccoli or cauliflower. Reserve a few small florets for garnish. In a large saucepan, fry 2 sliced onions in 30 g/1 oz butter until soft. Stir in 2 garlic cloves, add the stock and vegetables with salt and pepper to taste and bring to the boil. Purée the soup in a processor or with an immersion blender. Stir in 250 ml/8 fl oz double cream, bring back to the boil and season to taste again with salt and pepper. Serve hot with the reserved florets on top, or chilled with sour cream. Serves 4.

TURN INSIPID CORN KERNELS INTO CREAMED CORN

Transform insipid sweetcorn kernels into creamed corn: purée about half of the kernels using a processor or immersion blender and combine with remaining kernels in a saucepan. Add just enough double cream so the creamed corn falls easily from the spoon, heat until very hot and season to taste with salt, pepper, nutmeg and sugar.

TURN PALLID PEAS INTO
EASY ITALIAN RISI E BISI

If tasteless peas are your problem, make a quick version of Italian risi e bisi: for every 375 g/¾ pound cooked peas, bring an equal volume of chicken stock to the boil. Stir in 200 g/7 oz long-grain rice with salt and pepper. Cover and simmer 15-18 minutes or until all the liquid is absorbed and the rice is just tender.

Mcanwhile sauté 2-3 slices bacon, diced, in 1 tablespoon olive oil. Add the peas and heat 1-2 minutes. Stir the peas and bacon into the rice with 2 tablespoons chopped parsley. Taste and adjust the seasoning. Serves 4-6.

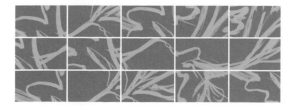

MOULD OVERCOOKED GREENS IN RAMEKINS WITH A CHEESY CUSTARD

When greens are seriously overcooked, chop them and mould in ramekins in a custard with grated cheese. Preheat the oven to 175°C/350°F/gas4. Drain the greens thoroughly. Coarsely chop them with a large knife. For every 375 g/¾ pound greens, butter four 250-ml/8-fl oz ramekins. Loosely pack the greens into the moulds. Whisk together 2 eggs, plus 2 extra egg yolks, 4 tablespoons each double cream and milk, 60 g/2 oz grated Parmesan cheese, ½ teaspoon grated nutmeg, salt and pepper. Pour the custard over the greens, making sure it soaks down the sides. Bake until the custard is firm and a skewer inserted in its centre comes out clean, 15–20 minutes. Serves 4.

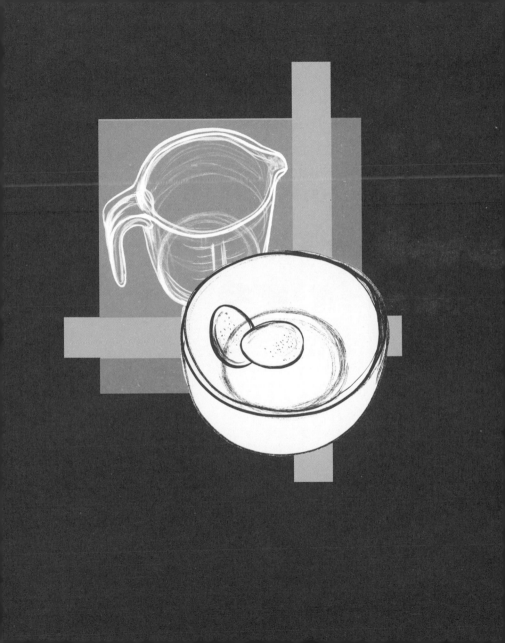

TIRED LETTUCE
MAKES GREAT SOUP

Make soup with chopped cooked lettuce. For every 250 g/½ pound, fry 1 sliced onion in 2 tablespoons olive oil until soft. Add the greens with 2 chopped garlic cloves and sauté for 1-2 minutes. Add about 1 litre/1⅔ pints stock, season and simmer until tender, 10-15 minutes. Stir in a drained 400-g/14-oz can of white kidney beans and bring to the boil. Stir in 30 g/1 oz shredded basil leaves. Serves 4.

MAKE MAURITIAN ROUGAILLE STEW FROM WATERY COURGETTES OR OTHER SQUASH

When squash, particularly courgette, is overcooked and watery, make rougaille (a Mauritian vegetable ragout). It is particularly good with rice and lentils.

For every 375 g/^{3}/4 pound cooked coarsely chopped squash, heat 2 tablespoons olive oil in a wok. Stir-fry 1 chopped onion until golden. Add the squash, 2 chopped garlic cloves and 1 teaspoon ground cumin, salt and pepper and fry over very high heat until dry, 3-5 minutes. Add 2 seeded, chopped tomatoes and fry for a minute or two. Stir in 2-3 tablespoons chopped coriander, and adjust the seasoning. Serves 4.

117

TURN LESS-THAN-PERFECT AUBERGINES INTO 'POOR MAN'S CAVIAR'

Providing the aubergine has not been mixed with too many other ingredients, give it new life by making Poor Man's Caviar.

Scrape the pulp from 4 medium aubergines (about 375 g/¾ pound) and discard the skins. Use a fork to mash up the aubergine with

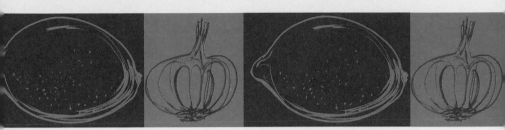

1 finely chopped garlic clove, 3 tablespoons lemon juice, 3 tablespoons olive oil, 2 tablespoons double cream, ½ teaspoon ground cumin, ½ teaspoon ground coriander, ½ teaspoon Tabasco sauce, salt and pepper. Taste, adding more Tabasco if you like. The mixture should be full flavoured and slightly chunky. Serve in a pretty pottery bowl with some salad greens or on toasted slices of country bread rubbed with garlic. Serves 4.

MAKE OVERCOOKED SWEET PEPPERS THE HEART OF A FILLING SPANISH OMELETTE

Overcooked peppers, with or without a stuffing, go well in a Spanish-style omelette.

For every 2 stuffed peppers or 375 g/ ¾ pound unstuffed, chop 2-3 tablespoons chopped coriander leaves. Very coarsely chop the peppers and stuffing and mix with the coriander. Dice 4 slices of bacon and fry until crisp and brown. Drain all but 2 tablespoons of fat from the pan, leaving the bacon. In a bowl. Whisk 4 eggs with salt and pepper until mixed. Heat fat and bacon until very hot, add eggs and stir briskly with a fork 30 seconds until they start to thicken at edges. Stir in vegetables. Continue cooking, pulling cooked mixture from edges to the centre of the pan with the fork, about 1 minute. When eggs are almost set, stop stirring and leave the omelette until firm and brown underneath, 2–3 minutes. Flip it on to a plate, slide it back into the pan and brown the other side, 2–3 minutes more. Serves 4.

FIVE CLEVER WAYS WITH OVERCOOKED TOMATOES

Creative outlets for overcooked tomatoes are legion and here are just a few. First peel away as much skin from the tomatoes as possible but you can leave the seeds. Then, choose one of the following:

• Coarsely chop the tomatoes, mix with chopped basil or flat-leaf parsley and add with olive oil to hot pasta or pasta salad.

- Drain chopped tomatoes and add to cornbread batter.
- Blend chopped tomatoes with cooked polenta or grits as a savoury accompaniment to meats or poultry.
- Make fresh or cooked tomato salsa (see pages 62 and 72).
- For a tomato sandwich, split a length of baguette, add tomatoes and drizzle with balsamic vinegar, salt and pepper; press sandwich between 2 heavy plates for at least 15 minutes, so all tomato juice is absorbed by the bread.

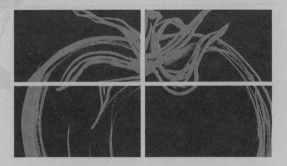

MAKE A RICH AND FLAVOURSOME PURÉE FROM OVERCOOKED ROOT VEG

The best solution for overcooked roots is puréeing. First spread on a baking sheet and heat in a 175°C/350°F/gas4 oven until dry, 5-10 minutes. Purée in a processor or with an immersion blender, for each 375 g/¾ pound of vegetable adding 60 ml/2 fl oz double cream and 2 tablespoons butter. If the vegetable is fibrous, work it through a sieve or food mill. Heat the purée in a saucepan, stirring, until very hot. It should fall easily from the spoon; if too stiff, add more cream. Season to taste with sugar, salt, pepper and spice of your choice. Serves 4.

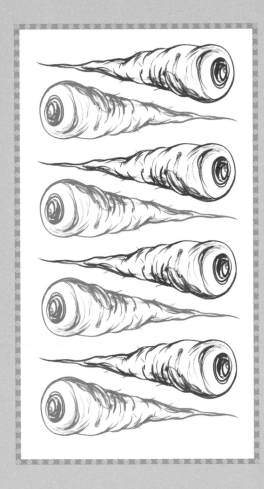

A HERB MASH TO USE UP OVERCOOKED OR FALLING-APART POTATOES

If potatoes are falling apart, take all the way by mashing with herbs. Drain well, return to pan and dry over low heat, 1-2 minutes. For each potato, add 3 tablespoons milk or cream, 15 g/$\frac{1}{2}$ oz butter and 1 tablespoon chopped herbs like chives or parsley. Beat over a low heat until fluffy. Season to taste.

A CRISP AND TASTY NUT TOPPING FOR BLAND ROAST ONIONS

When onion confit or baked onions are tasteless, add this crisp topping of spiced nuts.

Melt 60 g/2 oz butter in a pan over medium heat. Add 90 g/3 oz pecan halves or whole blanched almonds and toss until well coated. Add 1/2 teaspoon Worcestershire sauce, a large pinch each curry powder, ground ginger, salt and cayenne pepper to taste and toss again. Spread the nuts on a baking sheet and toast in a preheated 175°C/350°F/gas4 oven, stirring occasionally, until they are richly browned, 15-20 minutes; the spices may darken but will taste fine. Remove from the baking sheet and drain on paper towels. Coarsely chop the nuts and sprinkle on the onions. Serves 4-6.

ONION RINGS FOR CRUNCH
AND COLOUR

Onion rings make a quick, tasty garnish for all sorts of dishes and can help add crunch to many dishes that otherwise lack texture.

Thin rounds may be added raw to salads – look for mild, sweet onions that are often pink or purple in colour. Rings cut from more pungent yellow onions are delicious deep-fried. To cut an onion into rounds or rings: strip the skin, leaving the onion whole and trimming the root and stem. Turn the onion on its side, hold it securely on the board with one hand, and cut across into thick or thin slices using downward strokes. Leave the slices whole, or push them apart into rings.

To make crisp and fluffy fried onion rings for a delicious first course or to top steak or grilled vegetables: put separated rings from several large onions in a bowl of buttermilk to cover and chill for 15-30 minutes. Heat vegetable oil for deep-frying to 190°C/375°F in a deep-frying pan with a basket. Put 175g/6 oz flour in a large plastic bag with 1 teaspoon of salt and ½ teaspoon freshly ground black pepper, and shake to mix. Using your fingers, lift a generous handful of onion rings out of the buttermilk and add to the flour. Toss until lightly coated. Lift out the rings with your fingers, shake gently and drop into the hot oil. Fry for 1-2 minutes, stirring occasionally with a draining spoon, until lightly golden and crisp. Lift out in the basket, tip on to paper towels and leave to drain. Fry the remaining rings in the same way. They can be kept in a warm place for up to 15 minutes. Sprinkle them with salt just before serving.

GARLIC SOUP TO WARD OFF COLDS AND FLU

For a quick pick-me-up, try this fortifying garlic soup. In a medium saucepan, sauté 6 chopped garlic cloves in 1 tablespoon of olive oil until soft, about 1 minute. Add 1 litre/ 1⅔ pints water, the pared zest of 1 orange, 2 bay leaves, 2 sprigs each of thyme and rosemary, 1 whole clove, and salt and pepper to taste. Cover and simmer until the broth is very fragrant, 10-15 minutes. Traditional cooks do not strain the soup, but you may want to do so as the flavourings are not meant to be eaten. Serve at once, while still fresh and fragrant, with grated Parmesan cheese and crusty bread. For a more substantial soup, simmer a handful of vermicelli noodles or orzo in the broth just before serving. Serves 4.

TURN SECOND-RATE COOKED MUSHROOMS INTO A DELICIOUS SANDWICH OR OMELETTE FILLING

If mushrooms are dry or underflavoured, pour over some stock and simmer a minute or two until moist. Sprinkle with salt or soy sauce, pepper or fresh herbs, if you like. Makes a delicious filling for omelettes and sandwiches.

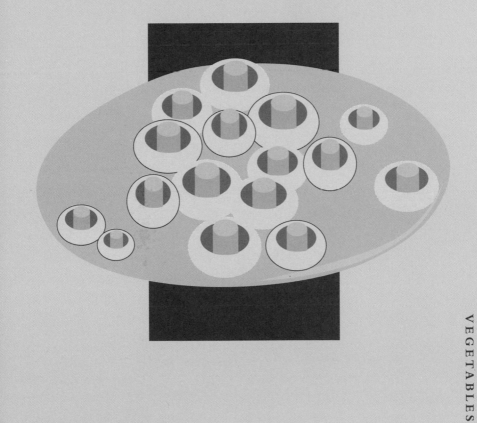

USE DISAPPOINTING STIR-FRIED VEG IN CHINESE OMELETTE CRÊPES

Use disappointing stir-fried vegetables in Chinese omelette crêpes: drain the vegetables well and coarsely chop them. For 375 g/ ¾ lb, finely chop 1 spring onion and 1 garlic clove. Whisk 4 eggs with seasoning until frothy. Oil a wok lightly and heat until the oil is just beginning to smoke. Off the heat, pour in 3-4 tablespoons egg, tilting to form a 13-cm/5-inch crêpe. Cook over high heat until brown, 1-2 minutes each side. Slide the crêpe on to a plate and cook the remaining crêpes in the same way, piling them to keep them warm. Heat more oil and stir-fry the spring onion and garlic for 1 minute. Add the vegetables and reheat rapidly, stirring, with soy sauce to taste. Wrap some in each crêpe. Serves 4.

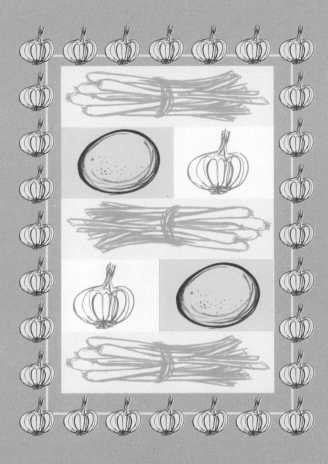

PERK UP BLAND DEEP-FRIED VEG WITH AN ORIENTAL DIPPING SAUCE

Deep-fried vegetables, particularly if bland, benefit from an Oriental dipping sauce:

whisk together 4 tablespoons water with 2 tablespoons each soy sauce, groundnut oil, red wine vinegar, sugar and sherry, with a pinch of red pepper flakes, 1 finely chopped garlic clove and a small piece of root ginger, finely chopped.

A DEEP-FRIED SHREDDED GINGER OR LEEK TOPPING SAVES BLAND BRAISED OR GLAZED VEGETABLES

When braised or glazed vegetables are soft or tasteless, top them with crispy deep-fried ginger or leek.

Thinly slice a 7.5-cm/3-inch piece of fresh ginger, cutting across the fibres. Taking a few at a time, stack the slices and cut those into the thinnest possible strips. For leek, cut 1 large leek into julienne strips. Heat oil for deep-frying to 190°C/375°F and deep-fry the ginger or leeks until crisp, 1–2 minutes. Lift out with draining spoon, dry on paper towels and scatter over the vegetables.

FAILSAFE WAYS OF IMPROVING ANY VEGETABLE PURÉE

Any purée is improved by adding butter and cream. For every 250 ml/8 fl oz purée, add 15-30 g/½-1 oz butter and 2-3 tablespoons double cream. Set the purée over medium heat and work with an immersion blender or beat by hand with a wooden spoon until the purée is light and smooth, 2-3 minutes. Add any of the following flavourings: allspice and cinnamon go well with pumpkin and squash, while summer vegetables like courgette, tomato and green beans better suit garlic and fresh herbs, such as oregano, basil and parsley.

USE OVERCOOKED VEGETABLES AS A GIANT SUBMARINE SANDWICH FILLING

Employ bland or overcooked vegetables as the filling of a giant submarine sandwich in a baguette loaf: brush the loaf with olive oil or vinaigrette dressing, and add the vegetables, layering them with sliced Gruyère or goats' cheese. Press the sandwich firmly together and cut in lengths at an angle for serving.

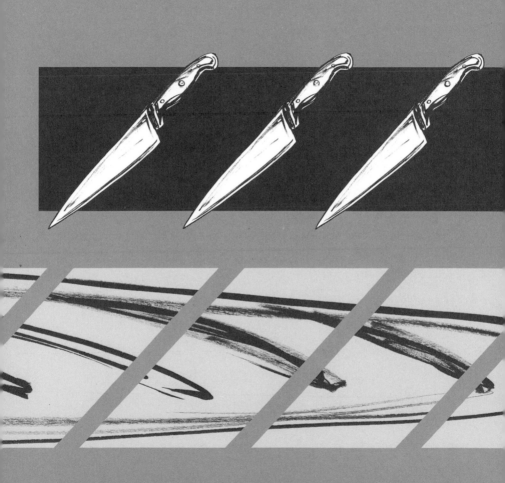

CLEVER WAYS TO SERVE OVER-SOFT VEGETABLE TERRINES

When a terrine or mould is seriously collapsed, bring bread to the rescue. Pack the mixture in pitta pockets with lots of crispy

beansprouts. For a party, pile the mixture on rounds of garlic bread and top with curls of Parmesan cheese or slivers of sun-dried tomato.

PASTA, GRAINS

& PULSES

DEALING WITH OVERCOOKED LONG PASTA

When pasta is seriously overcooked, start again – don't bother saving it as you'll always be disappointed. However, if the pasta is only slightly overdone, it's worth proceeding with the recipe. So the pasta does not tear, spoon sauce on top rather than tossing the two together, and don't forget the grated Parmesan!

RESCUING OVERCOOKED CANNELLONI OR LASAGNE

If baked cannelloni or lasagne are overcooked and dry, pour 250 ml/8 fl oz milk, stock or water over the pasta, then cover and continue baking briefly until the liquid is absorbed. Just before serving, sprinkle generously with freshly chopped herbs such as chives, basil or parsley.

153

THREE EASY WAYS OF IMPROVING LESS-THAN-PERFECT STUFFED PASTA

Here are three easy cover-ups for stuffed pasta that's less than perfect. Depending on the problem and the pasta, take your pick:

- Coat with a layer of tomato sauce.
- Fold in a few spoonfuls of double cream or crème fraîche.
- Top with crumbled crispy fried bacon.

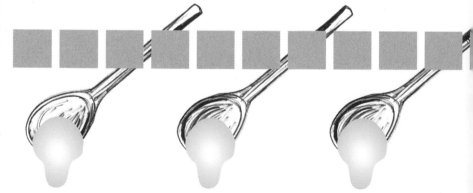

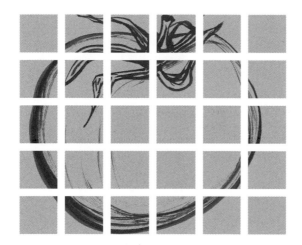

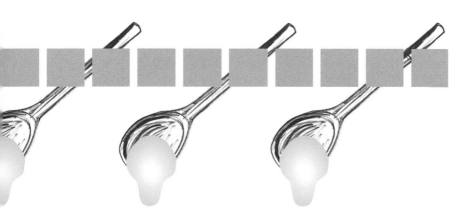

TURN OVERCOOKED OR BLAND RICE INTO A SIMPLE SAVOURY BAKE

When fluffy whole or cracked grains are overcooked or tasteless, save the day with savoury baked rice. Preheat the oven to 220°C/425°F/gas7. For every 500 g/1 pound

cooked grain, add 1 lightly beaten egg, 1 finely chopped garlic clove, 1 tablespoon chopped parsley, and plenty of freshly ground black pepper. Spoon the mixture into a buttered gratin dish and sprinkle with 2 tablespoons breadcrumbs. Dot with 30 g/ 1 oz butter and bake in the preheated oven until it is very hot and lightly browned, 12-15 minutes. Serves 2.

MAKE ITALIAN ARANCINI, OR CROQUETTES, FROM OVERCOOKED OR STODGY RISOTTO

Turn overcooked/sticky risotto into arancini or rice croquettes. Stir into 1 litre/1⅔ pints of the cold grain 2 lightly beaten eggs, 90 g/3 oz grated Parmesan cheese and 1 tablespoon chopped parsley. Divide the mixture into 12 equal portions and shape them into cylindrical croquettes. In a large frying pan, heat 2 tablespoons olive oil. Fry half the croquettes until golden brown, 2-3 minutes. Turn and brown other sides. Fry the remaining croquettes in the same way.
Serves 4-6.

TRANSFORM A STICKY OR BLAND PILAF INTO SPICED CAKES

When a grain pilaf is sticky or bland, transform it into spiced cakes.

For 1 litre/1$\frac{2}{3}$ pints pilaf, combine a 2.5-cm/1-inch piece of finely chopped fresh ginger, 2 finely chopped garlic cloves, 1 teaspoon aniseed and $\frac{1}{2}$ teaspoon each of ground cinnamon and cardamom. Stir in 125 ml/4 fl oz plain yogurt and grated zest and the juice of 1 lemon. Stir this mixture into the cold pilaf. Shape into 12 cakes. Brown the cakes in 2 tablespoons hot vegetable oil, allowing 2-3 minutes on each side. Serves 4-6.

WAYS OF RESCUING
STODGY POLENTA

When ground grains are heavy, you can smooth and lighten them with cream. Beat in single or double cream, adding just enough to thin the grain so that it falls easily from a spoon. Season well with salt, pepper and your choice of an aromatic spice such as coriander or cumin.

GIVE OVERCOOKED OR BLAND BEANS THE 'MEXICAN FRIED BEANS' TREATMENT

If beans are overcooked or tasteless, transform them into a version of Mexican fried beans.

Drain the beans and coarsely crush them. For every 1 litre/1⅔ pints of beans, dice 6 thin slices of bacon. Fry in a large frying pan until the bacon fat runs. Add 1 chopped onion, 2 crushed garlic cloves and, if you like, 1 small green chilli pepper, peeled, seeded and chopped. Continue frying, stirring, until both bacon and onions are brown. Stir in the crushed beans and cook, stirring constantly, until very hot, 5-7 minutes. Serves 6.

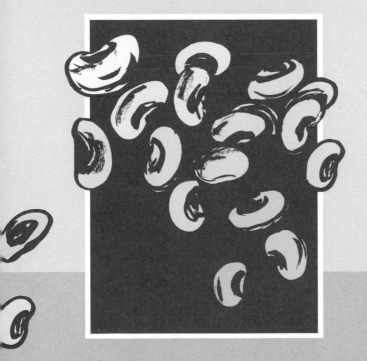

STOCKS &

SAUCES

THE EASIEST WAY TO SKIM OR DE-FAT HOT STOCK

Strips of paper towel are very useful for quick skimming, as well as removing any lingering fat globules from the hot stock by floating them on the surface.

LIFTING THE FLAVOUR OF ANY WHITE SAUCE

Milk has an affinity for nutmeg, and a generous grating of fresh nutmeg will improve the taste of any white sauce.

ADDING RICHNESS AND COLOUR TO A CHEESE SAUCE

If a cheese sauce lacks richness or colour, whisk in an egg yolk or two after adding the cheese, then taste for seasoning. Do not reheat the sauce or it will curdle.

TWO WAYS OF IMPROVING A VELOUTÉ SAUCE

A squeeze of lemon juice refreshes the flavour
of velouté, whether of fish, poultry or veal.
For richness and smooth texture, whisk in
double cream or crème fraîche.

IMPROVING BROWN SAUCES
AND GRAVIES WITH ALCOHOL

Madeira adds richness and colour as well as
flavour to a pallid sauce. For best results, add
several tablespoonfuls and simmer the sauce

for 5-10 minutes. Then whisk in a last tablespoon of Madeira to sharpen the flavour just before serving. Marsala can be used in the same way to give Italian richness, or you can use a mixture of port and Cognac.

EASY WAYS OF IMPROVING
ANY UNTHICKENED GRAVY

To disguise shortcomings, finish an unthickened gravy with some cream or butter. For every 250 ml/8 fl oz unthickened gravy, off the heat whisk in 1 tablespoon double cream or 15 g/½ oz butter.

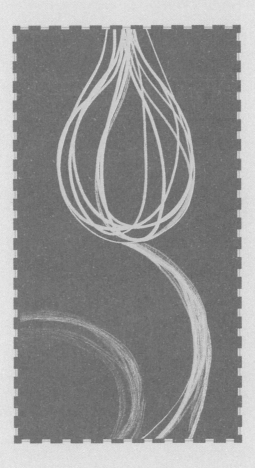

STOCKS & SAUCES

1 7 3

RESCUING CURDLED HOLLANDAISE SAUCE

When hollandaise curdles, the best remedy is to start again, using the curdled sauce in place of more melted butter. Whisk 1 egg yolk with a tablespoon of water over low heat to make a

light mousse which just holds the trail of a whisk. Take from heat and gradually whisk in curdled sauce, starting with a teaspoonful of sauce, then adding it more quickly once emulsion begins. Note: if the original sauce is severely overcooked so that egg yolk curds are cooked until firm, it cannot be saved.

RECONSTITUTING SEPARATED MAYONNAISE

When mayonnaise separates, it can be reconstituted. If the mayonnaise is cold to the touch, warm it to room temperature in a water bath. In a separate bowl, whisk a teaspoon of Dijon-style mustard with a pinch of salt, then gradually whisk in the separated mayonnaise as if it were oil, adding it drop by drop until the emulsion starts to form, then in a very slow stream. Note: be sure the emulsion forms and mayonnaise thickens from the very beginning.

DEALING WITH A SEPARATED BUTTER SAUCE

For 250 ml/8 fl oz separated butter sauce: in a separate saucepan, reduce 2 tablespoons double cream, whisking constantly, until thick, 1–2 minutes. Over a low heat, whisk 1 teaspoon of the broken butter sauce into reduced cream so it emulsifies. Whisk in 2–3 more spoonfuls, then whisk in the remaining sauce in a slow steady stream. Taste the sauce and adjust the seasoning. This fix does not have the staying power of a perfect sauce, but will hold up to 5 minutes without breaking.

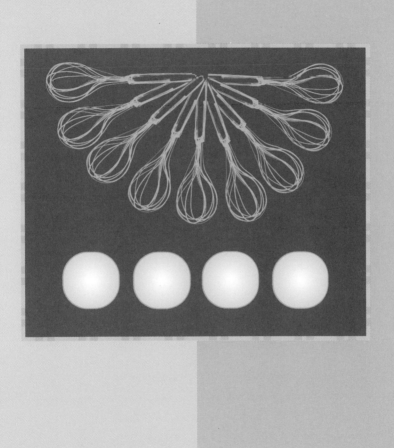

EMULSIFYING A THIN OR SEPARATED VINAIGRETTE

When a vinaigrette dressing is thin or separated, try whisking it vigorously by hand or with an immersion blender so the dressing emulsifies and thickens slightly. If this is not successful, start again in a small bowl with an emulsifier such as 1 teaspoon of Dijon-style mustard, 1 tablespoon of yogurt or double cream, or 1 very finely chopped shallot. Gradually whisk in the separated dressing, adding it slowly at first until an emulsion is established, then in a thin stream. Taste the dressing and adjust the seasoning.

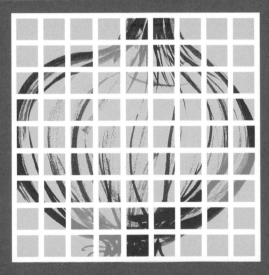

EMULSIONS
& EMULSIFIERS

An emulsion is formed when two substances
which would normally separate, for example
oil and vinegar, are combined to a smooth,
lightly thickened mixture. Sauces which rely
on an emulsion forming include mayonnaise,
hollandaise, béarnaise, white butter sauce, and
vinaigrette dressing.

Several factors help to create an emulsion.
One is to add an emulsifier – an ingredient
that helps other ingredients to combine in
this way. Common examples are egg yolks (in
hollandaise, béarnaise and mayonnaise),
Dijon-style mustard (in mayonnaise and

vinaigrette), the milk solids in butter and cream (in butter sauces), spices and herbs.

Next is vigorous whisking, typically adding one liquid to the emulsifier, starting drop by drop. It is crucial to establish the emulsion right at the beginning. Once off to a good start – you can tell by the slight but perceptible thickening of the mixture – the liquid may be added more quickly.

FIVE EASY WAYS OF IMPROVING SECOND-RATE TOMATO SAUCE OR SALSA

When tomato sauce or salsa is heavy or overcooked, or tastes flat, here are some simple additions. Choose whatever is appropriate to the dish:

- 125 ml/4 fl oz double cream.
- 2-3 seeded and chopped tomatoes.
- Enough red wine to restore the consistency you want.
- 2-3 tablespoons finely chopped celery and/or sweet onion.
- Adjust seasoning, particularly with lemon juice, vinegar, mustard, fresh herbs.

GIVING ZIP TO
A DREARY SALSA

When salsa seems dreary, try this remedy. First
drain off excess liquid. Next sharpen the taste
with citrus juice, particularly lime, then stir in
an aromatic chopped herb such as basil, dill or
coriander. Finally add zip with a splash of
Tabasco sauce.

SAVING A SLIGHTLY CURDLED CUSTARD SAUCE

If custard is slightly curdled, with a thin, coarse texture, emulsify it with an immersion blender, or work it in a blender until smooth. Note: if custard is so overcooked that firm curds of egg yolk have formed, nothing can be done.

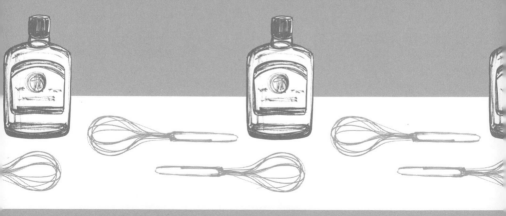

GIVING AN EDGE TO
DULL PASTRY CREAM OR
CUSTARD SAUCE

When pastry cream or custard sauce is heavy,
dull or tasteless, give it an edge by whisking
in 2-3 teaspoons kirsch or other white fruit
alcohol, with the grated zest of a lemon.

SAVING AN OVERCOOKED OR GRANULAR SABAYON

If sabayon overcooks and becomes granular, take it at once from the heat, set the bowl in cold water and whisk the sabayon until cool. Then transform it into a pleasant cream sauce. For every 250 ml/8 fl oz sabayon, whip 125 ml/4 fl oz double cream until it holds a soft peak. Fold the sabayon into the cream.

PERKING UP A THIN FLAT OR DISCOLOURED FRUIT COULIS

Pick up a coulis that is too thin, flat, pale or discoloured with chopped fresh fruit.

For each 250 ml/8 fl oz red berry coulis, stir in 175 g/6 oz coarsely chopped strawberries and raspberries and chopped mint; for each 250 ml/8 fl oz mango or peach coulis, add 175 g/6 oz chopped orange, honeydew or cantaloupe, with chopped lemon balm and toasted slivered almonds. The perfect disguise!

GIVING A FRUIT SAUCE THAT FINAL EDGE

After cooking, the flavour of a fruit sauce may need a pick-me-up such as a few drops of almond essence (good with plums, apricots and other stone fruits), or a teaspoon of vanilla essence or orange flower water.

WAYS OF IMPROVING CHOCOLATE SAUCE

There's nothing like a shot of alcohol for improving chocolate sauce: whisk in 1-2 tablespoons rum, whisky or brandy, adding it just before serving so the alcohol has no time to evaporate. Rather than throw the chocolate out, you may want to dissolve it in milk or cream and serve it as hot chocolate – allow about 250 ml/8 fl oz milk for 175 g/ 6 oz chocolate. The drink will, however, never be completely smooth.

RESCUING SEIZED OR STIFFENED MELTED CHOCOLATE

If chocolate seizes and stiffens suddenly during melting, take it from the heat and dry any beads of steam on the bowl; stir in 1-2 teaspoons vegetable oil or white vegetable fat, adding it a little at a time until the chocolate is smooth again – it will never be as glossy. Note: if very overheated, chocolate may be scorched and unusable.

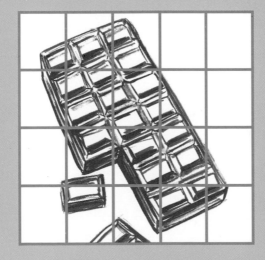

FRUIT

FRUIT

A SPICY SUGARY TOPPING FOR OVERCOOKED OR INSIPID APPLES

Revive apples which are overcooked or tasteless with a topping of spicy sugared nuts. In a medium frying pan, melt 30 g/1 oz butter with 1 teaspoon ground cinnamon and ¼ teaspoon ground ginger. Stir in 70 g/2⅓

oz coarsely chopped blanched almonds or walnut halves. Sauté over a medium heat, stirring the nuts until they start to pop showing they are toasted, 5-7 minutes. Remove the pan from the heat and stir in 2 tablespoons sugar. Spread the nuts out on a baking sheet and leave to cool. Sprinkle them over the apples just before serving. The topping serves 4.

THREE WAYS TO PEP UP POOR PEARS

If pears or quinces are bland or overcooked, take advantage of their affinity with peppy flavourings:

- Sprinkle them with freshly ground black pepper.
- Serve them with hot chocolate sauce (page 238).
- Make a quick fresh mint sauce: in a processor, purée 30 g/1 oz fresh mint leaves with 3 tablespoons raspberry vinegar and 3 tablespoons sugar. Using the pulse button, add 375 ml/12 fl oz double cream. Serve the sauce chilled for 4-6 people.

201

TOP DISAPPOINTING PLUMS OR APRICOTS WITH SPICED YOGHURT AND NUTS

Top disappointing, baked plums or apricots with spiced yogurt. Mix 1 teaspoon ground cardamom with 250 g/8 oz plain yogurt and 2 tablespoons brown sugar. Spoon over fruit and sprinkle with 3-4 tablespoons browned sliced almonds.

A SWEET-AND-SOUR SOLUTION TO SECOND-RATE CHERRIES

For tasteless or overcooked cherries, add a tablespoon or two of red wine vinegar or balsamic vinegar to the dish – a sweet-and-sour approach suits cherries very well.

REHABILITATING RHUBARB THAT'S OVERCOOKED OR OVERSHARP

When rhubarb is overcooked or unpleasantly acid, mix each 500 ml/16 fl oz of cooked fruit with 175 g/6 oz crushed meringues or macaroons. Whip 175 ml/6 fl oz double cream. Spread the fruit in a deep baking dish and top with the whipped cream. Serve chilled for 4-6.

A GINGER CREAM SAUCE TO SAVE DRY, PASTY OR OVERCOOKED BANANAS

For bananas which are dry, pasty or overcooked, prepare the following sauce: in a small bowl, whisk together 4 tablespoons lime juice, 1 tablespoon finely chopped fresh ginger and 2 tablespoons brown sugar. Gradually whisk in 250 ml/8 fl oz double cream. Spoon sauce over bananas or serve separately. Makes 375 ml/12 fl oz sauce to serve 4.

A CRISP CRUMBLE TOPPING FOR OVERCOOKED, WOOLLY OR BLAND PEACHES OR NECTARINES

Top overcooked, woolly or tasteless peaches or nectarines with a crisp crumble. For 500 g/1 pound fruit, in a food processor (or with

your fingers) work 90 g/3 oz butter to fine crumbs with 125 g/4 oz flour. Stir in 60 g/2 oz sugar. Drain the fruit, cut it in large chunks and spread it in a baking dish to form a 2.5-cm/1-inch layer. Spread the crumble on top and bake in a 230°C/450°F/gas8 oven until light golden and the fruit juice bubbles at the edges, 25-35 minutes. Serves 4.

MAKE OVERTART BERRIES PALATABLE IN A QUICK 'TRIFLE GRATIN'

When berries are overcooked or acid, make a quick 'trifle' topped with whipped cream browned under the grill. You'll need 250 g/8 oz sponge cake or biscuits, such as chocolate chip or oatmeal. Cut or break them into large chunks and spread in a soufflé dish or deep baking dish. Top with the berries and juice and leave until juice is absorbed. Stiffly whip 750 ml/24 fl oz double cream and spread over berries to cover them completely. Grill very close to heat for 3-4 minutes until cream melts and starts to brown. Serve at once for 4.

CARAMELIZE OVERCOOKED OR INSIPID FIGS

Grill overcooked or tasteless figs with brown sugar and cloves. For every 250 g/1⁄2 pound figs, mix 2 tablespoons sugar and 1⁄4 teaspoon ground cloves. Place the figs in a shallow flameproof baking dish and top with the sugar mixture. Grill until caramelized, 3-4 minutes. Serves 2.

THREE QUICK IDEAS FOR SAVING SECOND-RATE DEEP-FRIED FRUIT

A few fast ideas:
- In a food processor or blender, coarsely chop 2 tablespoons blanched whole or

sliced almonds or walnuts and 2 tablespoons brown sugar; sprinkle over fritters.

• Make a piquant dipping sauce by mixing 125 ml/4 fl oz white wine, 2 tablespoons lemon juice and 2 tablespoons honey. Stir in 2 tablespoons chopped raspberries or chopped dried cherries or cranberries. Serves 4.

• For soggy or undercooked fritters, spread fritters in a shallow baking dish, sprinkle with sugar and grill until tops are crisp and caramelized; serve with lemon wedges.

A SWEET-AND-SOUR GASTRIQUE TO SAVE POOR CHUTNEYS AND RELISHES

When chutney, confit or relish is bland, add a sweet-and-sour gastrique: for every 750 ml/24 fl oz conserve, heat 50 g/1⅔ oz sugar with 60 ml/2 fl oz water over low heat until

dissolved. Bring to the boil and boil without stirring to a dark golden caramel.

Take from the heat, let bubbles subside and add 75 ml/2½ fl oz red wine vinegar. Note: stand back as the vinegar vapour will otherwise sting your eyes. Heat gently, stirring until the caramel dissolves. Let cool, then stir the gastrique into the conserve.

PERKING UP THICK OR DULL JAM

When jam is thick or dull: just before using, stir in some chopped fresh raspberries, blackberries or peaches with a few tablespoons of raspberry or strawberry liqueur to soften the texture and pick up the taste.

GIVING A HERBAL TREATMENT TO FLAT OR BLAND JELLY

When jelly is bland or flat, put 2-3 leaves of a fresh herb in the jars, pour hot jelly on top and seal. The herb flavour will infuse the whole jar. Bay leaf, lemon verbena, mint, rosemary, sage and thyme are particularly good in this respect.

DESSERTS

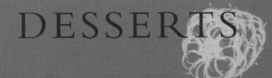

DESSERTS

CREAM CURDLES WHEN WHIPPING... MAKE IT INTO TASTY BUTTER

If cream curdles, you can always make butter: continue whipping it until the butter separates in clumps, 1-2 minutes. Transfer the butter pieces with a draining spoon to a bowl of cold water and squeeze with your fist to wash off whey, until the butter comes together into a single cake, 1-2 minutes. Lift out and dry on paper towels. If you like, sprinkle with up to $\frac{1}{2}$ teaspoon salt. Shape into a neat cake, wrap and chill; 500 ml/ 16 fl oz cream with 40 per cent butterfat yields about 150 g/5 oz butter.

SAVING SEPARATED EGG WHITES

When beaten egg whites have separated: for every 2 whites, add 1 unbeaten egg white and whisk very vigorously until smooth and light, about 45 seconds. Use at once.

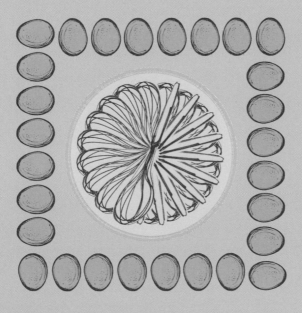

SAVING PROBLEMATIC BAKED CUSTARDS

Leave a problem custard in the mould. Sprinkle thickly with grated dark chocolate. If you like, add a layer of apple sauce. Top with whipped cream and sprinkle with a little more grated chocolate.

REVIVING BLAND OR HEAVY
BATTER PUDDINGS

If a batter pudding is bland or heavy, sprinkle
it while still warm with Cognac or rum – the
alcohol will vaporize and permeate the batter.
Orange or lemon juice is an alternative.

FOUR WAYS WITH IMPERFECT MERINGUE

A few ideas for imperfect meringues:

- Crumble meringue to layer with fresh fruit and sour cream flavoured with vanilla essence.

- Crumble meringues, top with crushed strawberries and hide them under a blanket of pastry cream or custard sauce flavoured with Grand Marnier and grated orange zest.
- Layer crushed meringues with ice cream as a moulded bombe.
- If meringues are too dark, hide the colour by dusting with icing sugar or cocoa.

ENLIVENING A DULL BREAD PUDDING

To enliven bread pudding, make rum or brandy butter.

Cream 90 g/3 oz of unsalted butter. Then add 75 g/2 $\frac{1}{2}$ oz sugar and beat until very soft and light, 2-3 minutes. Gradually beat in 3 tablespoons of rum or brandy. If the butter separates, set the bowl over warm water and beat again until smooth. Beat in the grated zest of 1 lemon. Chill the butter in the freezer until firm. Scoop it into balls for serving. Makes 175 g/6 oz to serve 4-6 people.

A 'BRÛLÉE' TOPPING TO JAZZ UP A ROUGH RICE PUD

If rice or a grain pudding is heavy or bland, top it with a thick layer of dark brown sugar and grill it until melted and caramelized.

A CARAMEL TOPPING TO LIFT A STODGY STEAMED PUD

When steamed pudding is heavy or undercooked, add a caramel topping: preheat the grill. Cut the pudding into 2-cm/ ¾-inch slices and set them on a buttered baking sheet. Sprinkle generously with granulated or brown sugar, spreading it evenly to the edge of the pudding. Grill until lightly caramelized, 3-5 minutes.

SAVING DISAPPOINTING SWEET FRITTERS

To save disappointing fritters: slice the fritters in half and set them on a baking sheet on paper towels. Warm them 3-5 minutes in a low oven. Fill them with tart jam or jelly to cut the richness.

BOOSTING THE FLAVOUR OF A DULL PRALINE

If a praline-flavoured mixture lacks flavour, the best approach is to boost the taste of almond.

Add Amaretto liqueur or just a few drops of almond essence (which is very concentrated).

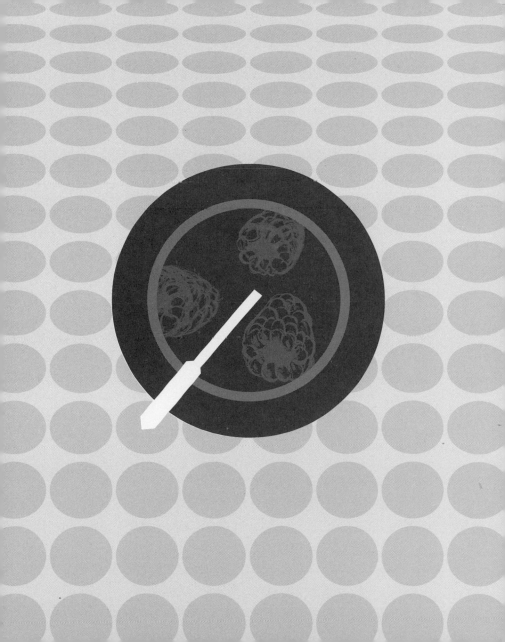

REMEDIES FOR A SUGAR SYRUP THAT STARTS TO CRYSTALLIZE

When a sugar syrup starts to crystallize before it caramelizes, add a tablespoon of honey and swirl the pan to mix. If still crystalline, take the pan from the heat and let cool slightly. Stir in a little water until the crystals dissolve, then continue boiling without stirring. If the crystals have formed a solid mass, start again with fresh sugar.

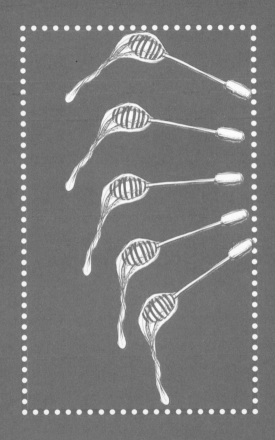

SANDWICH SECOND-RATE CRÊPES TOGETHER INTO A 'CAKE'

When crêpes are fragile or unevenly browned, sandwich them with whatever filling you have planned, laying them flat and piling in a tall stack. For savoury crêpes,

moisten with 3-4 tablespoons double cream, mixed with 1 tablespoon tomato purée if you like. For sweet crêpes, spoon over a glaze of 2-3 tablespoons honey heated until melted with the juice of 1 lemon. Bake crêpes in a 175°C/350°F/gas4 oven until browned and a skewer inserted in the centre is hot to the touch when withdrawn, 15-20 minutes.

TWO TOPPINGS TO PERK UP
BASIC BREAKFAST PANCAKES

When plain breakfast pancakes seem dreary, here are some quick toppings to pick them up:

- Make orange butter: cream 125 g/4 oz butter with 1 tablespoon icing sugar, 1 tablespoon orange juice and 1 tablespoon grated orange zest.

- For a creamy fruit sauce: whisk about 3-4 tablespoons raspberry jam or redcurrant jelly until soft. Whisk in 125 ml/4 fl oz double cream until smooth and thick.

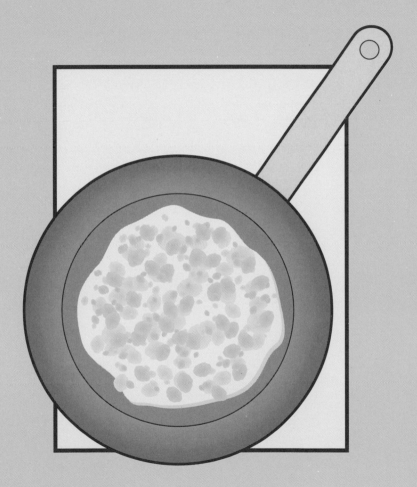

WAYS WITH PROBLEMATIC CHOCOLATE GANACHE

If the ganache is bland, beat in a few teaspoons of rum, Cognac or grated orange zest with sugar to taste, taking care not to soften texture with too much liquid. If the ganache seems bitter, add a generous spoonful or two of ground cinnamon. If the bland ganache has already been rolled into shapes, add cinnamon to the sugar or powdered cocoa used for coating.

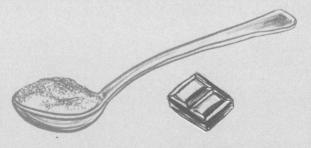

REMEDIES FOR IMPERFECT
CHOCOLATE TERRINES

If a terrine crumbles, make truffles: cut into rough
chunks. Dip the palms of your hands in icing sugar
or cocoa and roll chunks into rough balls. Drop
into chopped browned almonds or walnuts and toss
with forks until coated. Transfer to a baking sheet
and chill.

When a terrine is too soft to slice, scoop on crisp
cookies and set on individual plates. Top with
whipped cream and set another cookie flat on top
to make a sandwich.

FOUR WAYS TO USE A FAILED CHOCOLATE MOUSSE AS A TASTY SAUCE

When chocolate mousse does not set, or you are pressed for time, treat it as a rich chocolate sauce:

- Spoon it over vanilla ice cream.
- Layer it with fresh orange segments or chunks of pear in stemmed glasses and top with candied orange zest or a mint sprig.
- Serve it as a dipping sauce for strawberries.
- Make a swiss roll and use the chocolate mousse as the filling.

MAKING THE MOST OF A STIFF OR STRINGY JELLY

When a jelly is stiff or has strings when unmoulded, transfer it to a large sheet of wet greaseproof paper. Using a wet knife so the jelly does not stick, very coarsely chop it. For 1 litre/$1\frac{2}{3}$ pints chopped jelly, whip 250 ml/8 fl oz of double cream until it forms a soft peak. Fold the chopped jelly into the cream and spoon into parfait glasses. Chill thoroughly. Serves 4-6.

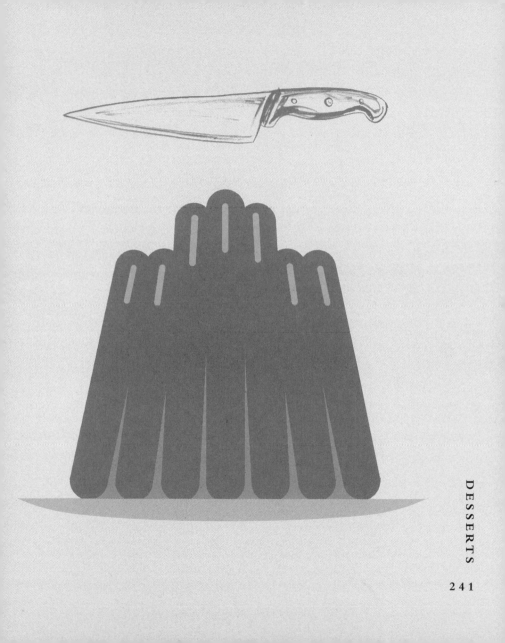

MAKE GRAINY OR INSIPID ICE CREAM INTO A VERSION OF PROFITEROLES WITH CHOCOLATE SAUCE

If ice cream is grainy or bland, make a simple version of profiteroles with chocolate sauce – almost any flavour of ice cream will do. To make the sauce: chop 175 g/6 oz dark chocolate and place in a pan. Bring 250 ml/8

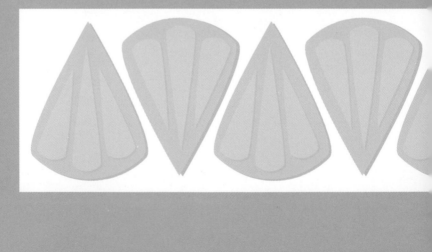

fl oz double cream just to the boil and pour it over the chocolate. Leave to melt for 2-3 minutes, then stir until smooth. Bring to the boil, stirring constantly, and simmer until lightly thickened, 1-2 minutes. Place 3 small scoops of ice cream in a triangle on 4 chilled plates (about 500 ml/16 fl oz ice cream). Prop 3 wafers upright between the scoops. Trail warm chocolate sauce over the ice cream and wafer and serve at once for 4.

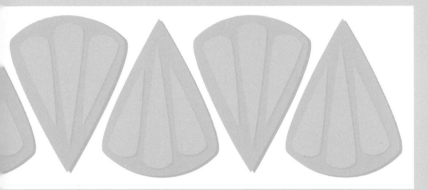

A KIWI SAUCE TO REVIVE A HEAVY OR BLAND SOUFFLÉ

This kiwi sauce will revive a heavy or bland soufflé or mousse, complementing most dessert flavours.

Peel 6 kiwi fruits, reserving 2 to slice for garnish. In a blender or food processor, purée the remaining 4 kiwis with 60 ml/2 fl oz white wine, 1 tablespoon of honey, and the juice and zest of 1 lime. Add 1 tablespoon of sugar or to taste and strain to remove the seeds. Spoon the mousse or soufflé on to individual plates, coat with sauce and top with sliced kiwi. Makes about 375 ml/ 12 fl oz sauce.

FLAMBÉED BANANAS TO
DISGUISE A POOR PARFAIT

When parfait is heavy or tasteless, top it with
flambéed bananas. For 4 people, peel and slice
2 bananas. Spoon the parfait into individual
bowls. Melt 30 g/1 oz butter in a frying pan,
add the bananas and sprinkle with

1 tablespoon sugar. Turn over the fruit and sprinkle with 1 more tablespoon of sugar. Sauté briskly until the sugar browns and caramelizes and the bananas are tender, stirring occasionally, about 2-3 minutes. Add 4 tablespoons rum or Cognac and flambé with a lighted match or by tipping the pan towards a gas flame. Baste the bananas, spoon over the parfait while still flaming and serve at once.

MAKE A SORBET THAT HAS CRYSTALLIZED INTO A GRANITA

If a sorbet is crystalline, serve it as granita: leave it to stiffen in the freezer, then stir with a fork to break up crystals. Pile in chilled stemmed glasses, layered with berries or sliced peaches if you like, and top with a mint sprig or twist of lemon zest.

BAKING

BAKING

FOUR HONOURABLE ENDS FOR LESS-THAN-PERFECT BREAD

Breadcrumbs, croûtes or toast are honourable ends for plain yeast breads:

- Fresh breadcrumbs: for very white crumbs, discard crust. If the bread is soft, freeze it. Tear it into pieces and purée a slice at a time in a food processor or blender. Store in the freezer. Use for stuffings.
- Browned breadcrumbs: toast the bread slices in a preheated 175°C/350°F/gas4 oven until dry and golden brown, 10-15.

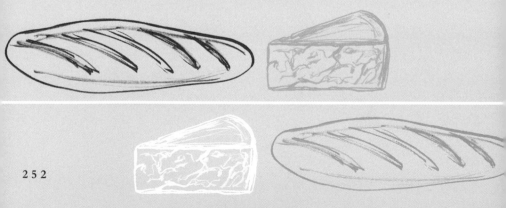

minutes. Purée as for fresh crumbs. Store in an airtight container. Sprinkle on gratins or baked dishes for colour and crunch.

- Croûtes: cut the bread into 1.25-cm/ ½ -inch slices and brush with melted butter, olive or vegetable oil; if you like, rub with a cut clove of garlic and sprinkle with grated cheese. If small, leave the slices whole, if large cut them in 4. Bake in a preheated l75°C/350°F/gas4 oven until crisp and lightly browned, 10-15 minutes.

- Melba toast: for a sandwich loaf. Cut bread into 1-cm/³⁄8-inch slices. Toast until light brown in a toaster. Discard crusts. Holding each slice flat with the palm of your hand, split it horizontally. Bake split slices in a preheated l75°C/350°F/gas4 oven until crisp and brown, 12-15 minutes.

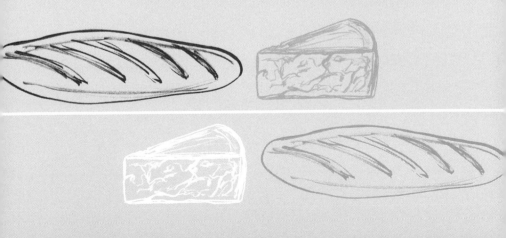

THE CRUCIAL CRUNCH OF CROUTONS

With a bit of imagination any leftover or dry bread can go a long way. Baked or fried croutons can be the backbone of simple broth soups such as chicken soup, French onion soup or garlic soup (page 132). Caesar salad is a pretty thin affair without hearty croutons seasoned with garlic, and a handful of crunchy croutons can make all the difference to a last-minute omelette.

To make herb croutons for 3-4 people: preheat the oven to 175°C/350°F/gas4. Discard the crusts from 4 thick slices of white or brown bread. Brush the slices generously with melted butter or olive oil. Cut the bread into 1.25-cm/$\frac{1}{2}$-inch cubes. Spread them on a baking tray and bake in the oven until lightly browned, stirring occasionally, about 8-10 minutes. Meanwhile, finely chop the leaves from 2-3 sprigs fresh thyme or sage and 3-4 sprigs of parsley. While the croutons are still warm, toss them with the herbs.

To make spiced croutons for 3-4 people: in a medium bowl, mix 1 teaspoon ground allspice or curry powder and $\frac{1}{2}$ teaspoon each of freshly grated nutmeg and freshly ground coriander. Cut 4 thick slices of white bread, including the crusts, into cubes about 1.25-cm/$\frac{1}{2}$-inch. In a large frying pan, melt 30g/1oz butter with 2 tablespoons vegetable oil, add the bread and fry briskly, stirring constantly, until the bread is browned, 1-2 minutes. Add to the spices and toss until the croutons are well coated.

USES FOR OVER-THE-HILL BAGUETTE

When baguette is over the hill, I make garlic bread: melt 125 g/4 oz butter with 2 chopped garlic cloves and 2 tablespoons chopped basil or parsley. Thickly slice a long loaf on the diagonal, leaving it joined at the base. Brush one side of each slice generously with butter. Bake in a 175°C/350°F/gas4 oven until crisp and fragrant, 10-12 minutes.

MAKE DRY SOURDOUGH OR WHOLEMEAL BREAD INTO BRUSCHETTA

Bruschetta is the answer for dry sourdough or whole-grain bread. Cut the bread into 2-cm/³⁄₄-inch slices and grill each side until browned. Brush with olive oil and rub with a cut garlic clove if you like. Add toppings such as thinly sliced prosciutto, peeled and sliced ripe tomatoes with shredded basil leaves, or sautéed chicken livers with onions and balsamic vinegar.

STALE BRIOCHE MAKES THE BEST FRENCH TOAST

With stale egg bread or brioche, make French toast. Trim the ends and cut 250 g/½ lb bread into generous 2.5-cm/1-inch slices. In a shallow bowl, combine 4 eggs with 250 ml/8 fl oz milk, 1 teaspoon cinnamon, ½ teaspoon vanilla essence and a pinch of salt. Whisk until well blended. Melt 15 g/½ oz butter in a large frying pan, dip the bread slices in the egg mixture to coat – do not soak long or the bread will become soggy. Taking care not to overcrowd the pan, fry the slices until golden brown, turning once, 1-1½ minutes. Add butter as needed and continue to fry the remaining slices. Serve at once with maple syrup, honey or a dusting of icing sugar.

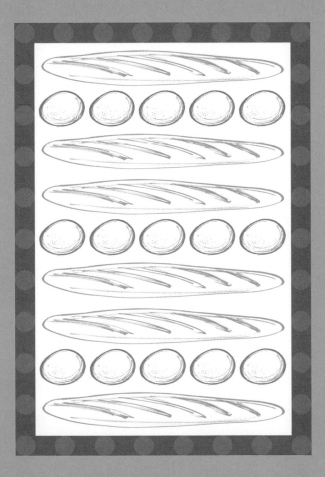

GIVING NEW LIFE TO
YESTERDAY'S CROISSANTS

Bakers recycle the previous day's croissants
this way: soften 125 g/4 oz prepared almond
paste with 1-2 tablespoons rum. Butterfly
4 croissants, splitting them not quite all the
way through the back. Spread them with
almond paste and grill until lightly browned,
2-3 minutes.

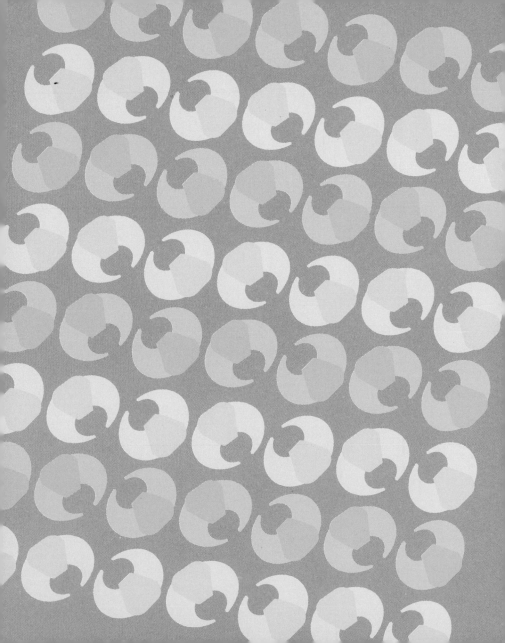

FIVE EMERGENCY RESCUES FOR LESS-THAN-PERFECT PIZZA

A handful of quick rescues for poor pizza:

- Sprinkle with crumbled goats' cheese or feta, or with grated Romano or Parmesan; grill if you like.
- Spread with spoonfuls of pesto or tapenade, or drizzle with a chilli- or herb-flavoured oil.
- Grind over generous amounts of black pepper.
- Add an orange gremolata – combine the finely chopped zest of 2 oranges, 2 finely chopped garlic cloves and 30 g/1oz chopped parsley.
- Arrange very thin slices of tomato all over the topping, sprinkle with grated cheese of any kind and grill until browned.

USING OLD FLAT BREADS TO MAKE TASTY STUFFINGS FOR POULTRY, PORK AND VEG

Most flatbreads make excellent light stuffings or toppings such as this aromatic herb and onion mixture for poultry, pork and vegetables. Tear 250 g/8 oz flatbread into pieces and purée to crumbs in a food

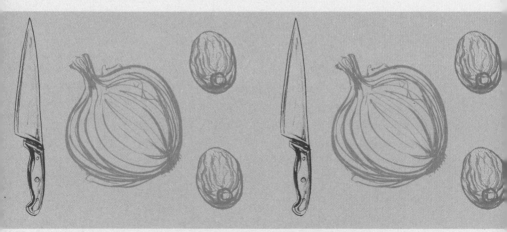

processor or blender. Sauté 4 chopped
medium onions in 2-3 tablespoons butter or
vegetable oil until soft but not brown. Let
cool, then stir in the breadcrumbs with
125 ml/4 fl oz stock, 3 tablespoons chopped
coriander or mint leaves, 1 teaspoon ground
coriander and ½ teaspoon grated nutmeg.
Season to taste with salt, pepper and more
nutmeg. For stuffing, stir in 2 lightly beaten
eggs to bind the mixture. Makes about
500 g/1 lb stuffing.

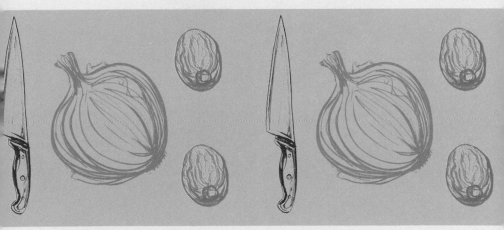

THREE WAYS TO SAVE DRY
SCONES OR TEA BREADS

Dry scones and tea breads are easily
improved:

- Use them American-style with a main
  meal, moistened with a spoonful of gravy,
  or float them in buttermilk.
- Split scones, top the halves with sliced
  cheese and grill them.
- Slice tea breads thinly, spread with butter
  and grill until toasted.

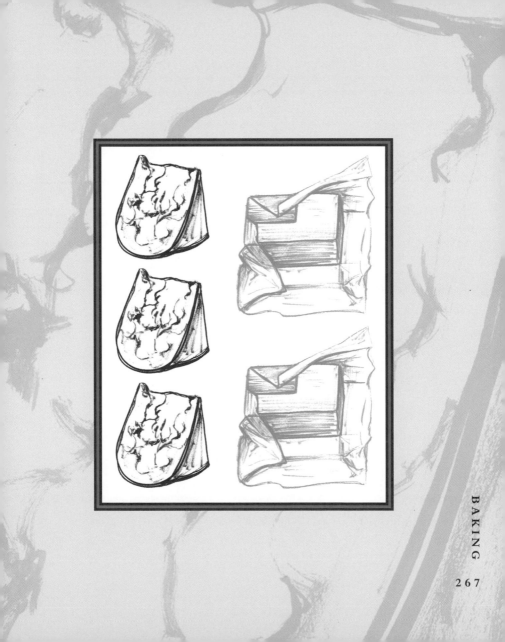

MAKE RUM BALLS FROM
HEAVY OR STALE MUFFINS

If muffins are heavy or stale, make rum balls:
for every 175 g/6 oz of muffins, finely chop
125 g/4 oz walnut halves with the muffins in
the food processor. Sift together 125 g/4 oz

icing sugar and 2 tablespoons cocoa. Stir in 4 tablespoons rum and 1 tablespoon light corn syrup or honey. Stir in the crumb mixture – it should be moist enough to shape. Roll the mixture between the palms into walnut-sized balls. Set on a tray of icing sugar and roll with two forks until coated. Makes about 40 balls.

WAYS OF SAVING HEAVY OR DRY SPONGE CAKE

If a sponge cake is heavy, dry, or unevenly baked:

- Split the cake horizontally and brush with syrup made with 60 g/2 oz sugar dissolved in 3 tablespoons water and then flavoured with 2 tablespoons Cognac; add a fruit mousse or other filling of fruit and cream.

- Serve the cake with this orange sauce: with a serrated knife, cut the skin and pith from 3 oranges; cut out the orange segments, discarding the membranes and reserving any juice. Melt about 4 tablespoons of orange marmalade in a small pan. Stir in 125 ml/4 fl oz orange juice, including the reserved juice from the oranges. Let cool, then stir in the orange segments and 1 tablespoon Grand Marnier. For greater effect use blood oranges; makes 250 ml/8 fl oz sauce.

USE HEAVY ANGEL FOOD CAKE IN A SWEET CARAMEL FONDUE

If angel food cake is heavy or sticks to the pan, cut the cake in large cubes and serve as a

fondue with a caramel sauce (page 290) for dipping. For lightness, you can also add some fresh strawberries.

If a creamed cake is heavy or underbaked, cut it in thick slices and brown in a toaster or under the grill. Top with jam or ice cream.

USES FOR A FALLING-APART SWISS ROLL

If cake for a Swiss roll cracks badly or sticks, make triple-decker towers: cut 7.5-cm/ 3-inch rounds with a biscuit or pastry cutter, allowing 3 rounds per person. Reserve the best rounds for topping. Sandwich and top 2 remaining rounds with your filling, piping rosettes if possible for neat effect. Hide trimmings of cake inside the filling. Cut the reserved rounds in half and perch them at an angle on the filling, like butterfly wings. Leave plain, or decorate with a 'body' of red berries or a single chocolate truffle.

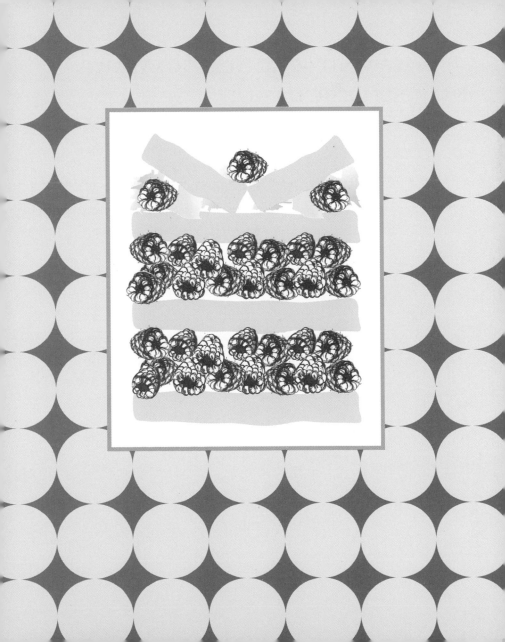

SAVING STALE LEFTOVER SLICES OF FRUIT CAKE

Slice dry or leftover pieces of fruit cake and sauté in butter until hot. Serve at once with brandy butter.

MAKE DRY GINGERBREAD INTO ICE CREAM

If gingerbread or a spice bread is dry, use it to flavour ice cream: break it by hand or in a food processor to coarse crumbs. For every 250 g/8 oz crumbs, allow 1 litre/1⅔ pints vanilla ice cream. Leave the ice cream to thaw until slightly soft. Toast the crumbs in a 175°C/350°F/gas4 oven until dry and crisp, 10–15 minutes. Stir into the ice cream and taste, adding more spice such as ground ginger or cinnamon if you like. Refreeze the ice cream until firm.

A CARAMEL FROSTING TO TOP OVER-HEAVY TORTES

If very dense, top a torte with fluffy caramel frosting: in a large bowl, combine 150 g/5 oz dark brown sugar and 2 egg whites. Set over a pan of simmering water and beat until the frosting stiffens and holds a long peak, 5-7 minutes. Take from heat and beat until tepid, 1-2 minutes. Beat in 1 teaspoon vanilla essence and spread on the cake, swirling it into peaks – the frosting will harden on standing. Enough for a 25-cm/10-inch torte.

TURN LESS-THAN-PERFECT CHEESECAKE INTO A TASTY MOUSSE

When underbaked cheesecake sinks badly or collapses, refurbish it as a mousse to serve with gingersnap biscuits or fresh fruit.

Scoop the cheesecake from the pan, leaving as much crust as possible behind. For every 600 ml/1 pint underbaked batter, beat in 2 lightly whisked egg whites, using a mixer to obtain a stiff, smooth mixture. Taste and, if you like, add a dash of rum. Whip 125 ml/ 4 fl oz double cream and fold into the mixture. Pile the mousse in bowls and chill. Serves 4-6.

MAKING PASTRY CASES FROM HARD-TO-ROLL PASTRY

If pastry is hard to roll, making lining a pan difficult, or if a shell has collapsed in the oven and lost its sides, make a flat pastry round. Trim the edges of the raw or partially cooked pastry to a neat round, the same size as a ceramic quiche dish or heatproof glass pie plate. Bake this pastry round completely at the same heat as the case. Add the filling to the quiche dish or pie plate and bake without pastry. For serving, top the filling with the pastry round, or cut the pastry into wedges to serve separately.

DISGUISING DAMAGED TARTLETS

If a tartlet sticks or collapses, hide the damage with a frivolous decoration of herbs or edible flowers.

HIDE POOR QUICHE UNDER
A LAYER OF MELTED CHEESE

Improve soggy or overcooked quiche by hiding it under a layer of melted cheese.

For a 25-cm/10-inch quiche, combine about 100 g/3¼ oz grated Gruyère, 50 g/1¾ oz chopped celery and 3-4 tablespoons chopped parsley. Spread the cheese topping on the quiche and season the topping generously with freshly ground black pepper. Bake at 230°C/450°F/gas8 until the cheese is melted and browned, 8-10 minutes.

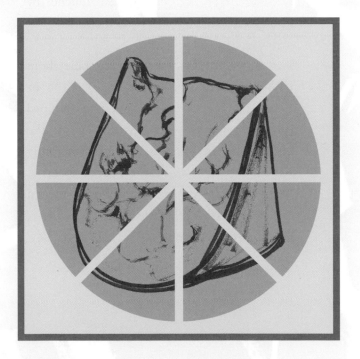

A LIVELY LEMON SAUCE TO PERK UP A SAD FRUIT PIE

Serve a disappointing fruit pie with this lively lemon sauce, a sweet version of Greek *avgolemono*.

Bring 250 ml/8 fl oz double cream to boil. Whisk together 3 egg yolks, 1 tablespoon of sugar and the juice of 1 lemon. Pour in the hot cream, whisking constantly. Return the sauce to heat and cook gently, stirring constantly, until it thickens slightly. Note: do not boil or it will curdle. Makes about 375 ml/12 fl oz, to serve 4-6.

WAYS OF COVERING UP
MESSY PASTRY

If puff pastry looks a mess, add small bouquets of greens and edible flowers, draping them to hide the misery. If heavy, soggy or lacking flavour, add distracting flavourings such as chopped herbs, olives, red or green pepper, lemon juice and Cognac or Madeira to accent the filling.

Sprinkle less-than-perfect savoury puff pastries with grated cheese and continue baking until melted; sprinkle sweet puff pastries with more sugar if needed and continue baking until well caramelized.

MAKING GOOD USE OF
DEFLATED CHOUX PUFFS

When sweet puffs have fallen and cannot be filled, sandwich filling between two puffs, adding raspberries or other fruit if you like. Place the puffs on plates. Make a caramel: heat 200 g/6½ oz sugar with 125 ml/4 fl oz

water until dissolved, stirring occasionally. Bring to the boil and boil without stirring to a deep golden caramel. Take the pan from the heat and plunge the base in a pan of warm water to stop cooking. At once trail warm caramel over the puffs in a lattice. The caramel will set to be crisp as it cools.

REVIVING TIRED LAYERED PASTRIES

When sweet or savoury layered pastries seem tired, cut them into individual portions and set them spaced apart on a baking sheet. Bake in a moderate 175°C/350°F/gas4 oven until very hot and the edges are crisp, 10-15 minutes.

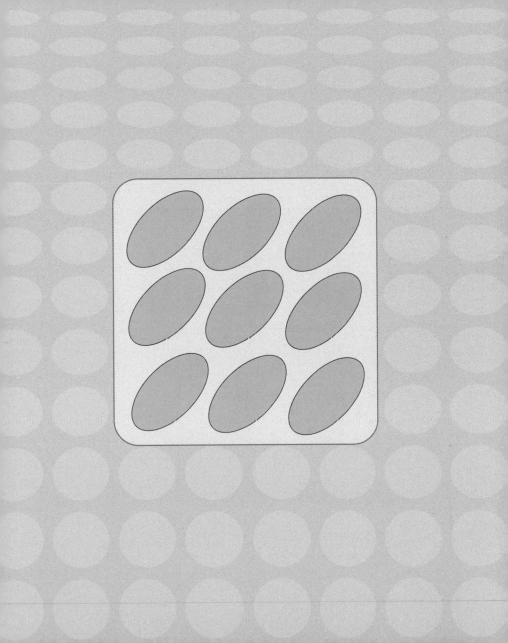

A CREAM CHEESE SAUCE TO DISGUISE OVERCOOKED OR HEAVY PASTRY PARCELS

When savoury layered pastry parcels are scorched or heavy, add this sauce: in a food processor combine 125 g/4 oz soft cream cheese with 30 g/1 oz chopped tarragon or parsley, 1 tablespoon whole-grain mustard and enough sour or double cream to make a pourable sauce. Taste for seasoning. Serves 4.

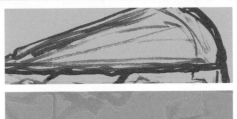

A TART ICING
TO PERK UP
BLAND BISCUITS

When biscuits are bland or need a pick-me-up, add this tart icing: beat 125 g/4 oz sifted icing sugar with the grated rind and juice of 1 orange until smooth. The icing should just fall easily from the spoon – if too thick, add more orange juice; if too thin, beat in more sifted icing sugar. Brush a teaspoonful or so of icing on each biscuit, leaving it to spread and set when cool. Makes 75 ml/2½ fl oz, enough for about 24 biscuits.

JAZZING UP BORING DROP BISCUITS

When drop biscuits are dry or plain, let them cool and dip one edge in your choice of melted chocolate – dark, milk or white. Place them to cool and set on greaseproof paper.

RECRISPING SOGGY WAFERS

When tiles or wafer biscuits are soft, dry and crisp them in the oven, then reshape them: heat the biscuits on a baking sheet in a l75°C/350°F/gas4 oven for 4–5 minutes. They will collapse and become pliable. Reshape them while still hot and leave to cool.

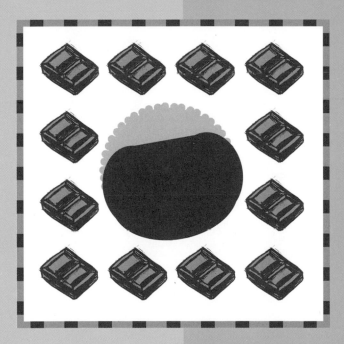

INDEX

ACKNOWLEDGEMENTS

I would like to extend warmest thanks to Virginia Willis, who has been my right hand in bringing this material to fruition. My other leading associates in the kitchen, on the studio floor, and at the editorial desk, have been Chefs Alexandre Bird and Laurent Terrasson, together with Kevin Tyldesley, Val Cipollone and Marah Stets. I have also had valuable help at different times from Ken Atkinson, Tim Furst, Lin Hansen, Amanda Hesser and Bongani Ngwane. That's only half the story. There is also the team from Quadrille Publishing in London. I would like to acknowledge all those named below, particularly my editor Lewis Esson, who from start to finish worked with us so long and hard on this project.

This edition published in 2005 by Quadrille Publishing Limited, Alhambra House, 27-31 Charing Cross Road, London WC2H OLS

Based on material originally published in *Cooked to Perfection*

Editorial Director: Jane O'Shea
Creative Director: Helen Lewis
Editor & Project Manager: Lewis Esson
Illustrations: Janet Simon
Design: Paul Welti
Design Production Service: Keith Holmes, Redbus
Production: Rebecca Short

Text © Anne Willan Inc. 1997 & 2005
Illustrations © Janet Simon 2005
Edited text, design & layout © Quadrille Publishing Ltd 2005

Cataloguing in Publication Data: a catalogue record for this book is available from the British Library

ISBN 1 84400 201 2

Printed and bound in China